Mexican Guerrillas, Domestic Elites, and the United States of America

1846–1848

Irving W. Levinson

Library of Congress Cataloging-in-Publication Data

Levinson, Irving W.
 Wars within war : Mexican guerrillas, domestic elites, and the United
States of America, 1846-1848 / by Irving W. Levinson.
    p. cm.
 Includes bibliographical references.
 ISBN 0-87565-302-2
 1. Mexican War, 1846-1848. 2. Mexican War, 1846-1848—Social
aspects. 3. Mexican War, 1846-1848—Mexico. 4. Guerrillas—Mexico—
History—19th century. 5. Elite (Social sciences)—Mexico—History—
19th century. 6. Mexico—History, Military—19th century. 7. Mexico—
Politics and government—1821-1861. 8. Mexico—Social conditions—
19th century. I. Title.
 E404.L49 2005
 973.6'2—dc22
                        2004017279

Printed in Canada

TABLE OF CONTENTS

ACKNOWLEDGMENTS

In 1995, Dr. Edward Countryman told me, "No one ever truly writes history alone." In that year, I did not fully understand the meaning of his words. Now, after seven years as a historian, I do. This project was born through the efforts of many individuals; they deserve both this written acknowledgment as well as my deepest appreciation.

Dr. John Mason Hart, University of Houston, proved to be an exemplary mentor, guide, and critic for my work. His exceptional knowledge of México's history and archives enabled me to achieve far more than would otherwise have been the case. Dr. Hart's enthusiasm for his colleagues and their work remains constant.

Dr. Thomas F. O'Brien, Dr. James Kirby Martin, and Dr. R. Andrew Chesnut provided vigorous analysis of my work, and Dr. Fred Schiff offered valuable observations from his perspective as a sociologist. Dr. Joe Glaathaar, noted military historian, was the source of much good counsel during the research phase of my work. These scholars gave unstintingly of their time, and I am indebted to them.

In Mexico City, Colonel José Manuel Zozaya Gallegos earned my deepest appreciation. His decision to grant my petition for access to the *Archivo de la Defensa Nacional* in Mexico City enabled me to review some extraordinary source materials. His willingness to grant me broad access to documents about a period that still arouses the deepest sentiments both north and south of the Río Bravo (Rio Grande) represents the highest traditions of our profession.

In several respects, the colonel's facility proved exceptional. The skills of his staff in preserving materials may be judged by one statistic: Of the

12,086 pages I reviewed, only two had suffered deterioration. The cataloguing efforts of current and previous Defensa staff produced a chronological listing of the archive's holdings grouped into thousands of folders, each of which had splendidly specific titles often running to ten or more lines. The lieutenant, sergeants, corporals, and privates with whom I worked on a daily basis consistently aided my efforts and repeatedly demonstrated their deep knowledge of and enthusiasm for their nation's history and heritage. Also, I did not see a single frown or hear one raised voice during almost a year of work in their archive. *Que les vayan bien.*

In Xalapa, Licensado Antonio Riquelme graciously provided full access to the extraordinarily detailed records kept by that community's *cabildo* (municipal council) during 1845–49. The hours I spent in the sunny, breezy high-ceilinged chamber that serves as the municipal archive's reading room remain among my most pleasant memories of México. Also, Licensado Riquelme is the only archivist of my acquaintance in either nation who provides his guests with classical radio music to drown out any street noise.

American archivists also provided exceptional support. At the National Archives and Records Administration, in Washington, D.C., Mr. Michael Musick suggested several additional avenues of research, each of which proved to be highly rewarding. Mr. David Keough provided a similar level of assistance at the U.S. Army Military Institute in Carlisle, Pennsylvania. He and his colleague, Dr. Richard Somers, thoroughly enjoy history and welcomed the opportunity to discuss my topic, making several valuable suggestions.

Sooner or later, all U.S. scholars of Latin America journey to the University of Texas' Benson Latin American Collection. For me, as for so many others, a search of the library's collection yielded splendid treasure.

Although all of the staff with whom I worked in Austin unfailingly provided excellent assistance, I owe a particular debt to Carmen Sacomani. She not only possesses a unique depth of knowledge of the archival material at the Benson, but also of materials at other leading facilities in North America.

J. W. Fulbright Scholarship Commission funds enabled me to review far more material than otherwise would have been the case. In Mexico City, that agency's affiliate organization, the Fulbright-García Robles Program, helped with many details. Two of its staff, Omi Kerr and Sara Levy, deserve the admiration and friendship of all who work with them. My research in the United States received substantial support from the University of Houston History Department's Murray Miller Scholarship Program, allowing me to conduct research at the National Archives and Records Administration in Washington, D.C.; at the Library of Congress; and at the U.S. Army Military History Institute.

My only remaining acknowledgment concerns errors—any that you may encounter in this text are mine and mine alone.

Photographs, Tables, and Maps

LIST OF ARCHIVAL ABBREVIATIONS

ACDN	Archivo de Cancelados de la Defensa Nacional, Mexico City
ADN	Archivo de la Defensa Nacional, Mexico City
AGN	Archivo General de la Nación, Mexico City
AHEM	Archivo Histórico del Estado, Toluca, México
AHAO	Archivo Histórico del Ayuntamiento, Orizaba, Veracruz
AHEO	Archivo Histórico del Estado, Oaxaca
AHEV	Archivo Histórico del Estado, Xalapa, Veracruz
AHMX	Archivo Histórico del Municipio, Xalapa, Veracruz
AHMT	Archivo Histórico Municipal de Toluca de Lerdo, Toluca, México
AHSRE	Archivo Histórico de la Secretaría de Relaciónes Exteriores, Mexico City
ASM	Archivo del Senado de México, Mexico City
BIM	Biblioteca Instituto Dr. José Maria Luis Mora, Mexico City
BLAC	Benson Latin American Collection, University of Texas, Austin
BMLT	Biblioteca Manuel Lerdo de Tejada, Mexico City
BNM	Banco Nacional de México, Mexico City
CEHM	Centro de Estudios de Historia de Mexico (CONDUMEX), Mexico City
FRBN	Fondo Reservado y Biblioteca Nacional, Mexico City
GMWH	Gilcrease Museum of Western History, Tulsa, Oklahoma
HNM	Hemeroteca Nacional de México, Mexico City
LCMSS	Library of Congress, Manuscripts Section, Washington, D.C.
MMOB	Mapoteca Manuel Orozco y Berra, Mexico City
NARA I	National Archives and Records Administration, Washington, D.C.
NARA II	National Archives and Records Administration, College Park, Maryland
USAMHI	United States Army Military History Institute, Carlisle, Pennsylvania

INTRODUCTION

History knows no resting places and no plateaus.

HENRY KISSINGER

Some forty-one miles west of Mexico City lies the state capital of Toluca de Lerdo. On January 18, 1848, that community's city council met in a time of war. During the council's discussion about a group of local citizens who recently left the city to wage partisan warfare against the United States Army, the legislators noted that these volunteers were not fighting those invaders. Instead, they had joined forces under the command of General Juan Álvarez, who was combating other Mexicans then in rebellion against the federal government. Without surprise, council members acknowledged that Mexicans waged war against each other while a foreign army of occupation held the nation's nearby capital.[1]

Traditional characterizations of the 1846–48 war as a conflict between two sovereign states pay only slight heed to such events. Such histories provide a flawed record of that conflict; several wars took place during these years.

The longest and most important of these conflicts was among Mexicans. This clash consisted not of the occasional coups that flared into existence at several points during the war, but reflected the older struggle between a predominantly *criollo* elite that claimed European or "white" parentage and the majority of the population that was forcibly excluded from meaningful participation in the nation's political and economic life.

In its various manifestations, this conflict remains a crucial factor of Mexican history. Each of the more prominent and violent episodes in this age-old struggle bears a different name. From 1842 to 1845, members of indigenous tribes, peasants, and residents of communal villages living in a sixty–thousand–square–mile swath of territory in southwestern México launched the Álvarez Rebellion. From 1845 to 1853, a rebellion of the

As proved to be the case with many other Mexicans, Álvarez's cooperation in the war against the U.S. Army was less than wholehearted. In later years, he waged war against Santa Anna.
    Carlos Guevara. General Juan Álvarez, 19th Century. Oil on canvas. Museo Nacional de Historia. Reproducción Autorizada por el Instituto Nacional de Antropología e Historia.

Maya known as the Caste War erupted throughout the Yucatán peninsula. During the Mexican Revolution of 1910–16, Emiliano Zapata led a peasant army in the state of Morelos to military victories against both the *ancien régime* of President Porfirio Díaz and against post-revolutionary forces commanded by Venustiano Carranza. The rebellions waged by many Mexicans and by some military officers against their nation's government during the 1846–48 period also belong on this list.

These rebels mounted campaigns in many areas of the nation. In the states of Baja California, Hidalgo, Puebla, México state, and Veracruz, they violently challenged their governments before, during, and after the invading army of General Winfield Scott marched inland to Mexico City. In the Yucatán and in Chiapas, Guanajuato, and Querétaro, agrarian and ethnically based movements also erupted to challenge state authority. Guerrilla groups hostile to the regime in Mexico City repeatedly forced the national government to divert military resources away from the conflict with the United States and toward the restoration of state authority. The Mexican elite's urgent desire to control these rebellions constituted a crucial factor in their decision to accept the provisions of the Treaty of Guadalupe Hidalgo.

Many of México's most powerful and propertied citizens evinced a greater fear of their fellow Mexicans than of the invaders from the north. Indeed, at critical moments during the 1846–48 period, elements of that national elite turned to the U.S. Army for both armaments and manpower in confronting these domestic challenges to their authority. By presenting their rulers with such a powerful challenge and by consequently forcing México's government to abandon any consideration of further resistance to the United States, these guerrillas changed the course of the war and Mexican history.[2]

Another conflict took place during the 1846–48 war. In that struggle, the U.S. Army fought partisan groups sanctioned by the Mexican government as well as forces beyond the control of the administration in Mexico City. By their actions, these two guerrilla forces altered the perceptions and goals of major U.S. civilian and military officials. Those senior authorities deemed the difficulties of an extended occupation of México so significant that they grew to prefer a rapidly concluded treaty to previous objectives, such as the annexation of the states of Sonora and Chihuahua, as well as parts of Coahuila, Nuevo León, and Tamaulipas. The dilemmas posed by partisans grew to the extent that a senior U.S. commander, General Zachary Taylor, advocated a unilateral withdrawal to the Rio Grande–Alta California boundary. In bringing about this change of sentiment, guerrillas once again changed the course of the war.

This reality directly contradicts the frequent assertion that the partisans' military significance gradually diminished following successive U.S. victories against them at Puebla (October 1847), Las Vigas (June 1847), Las Animas (August 1847), and Sequalteplán (February 1848). In the new paradigm of this conflict, the balance between victory and defeat rested not only upon the outcomes of the major battles between the regular armies of the two nations, but upon the actions of the guerrillas and upon the responses made by the millions of Mexicans who found an invading army of barely twelve thousand men marching through their midst and on to Mexico City in 1847. Those civilians who decided to absent themselves from any participation in the conflicts as well as those who did participate influenced the course of events.

To understand the Mexicans' actions, we need to know the framework through which they viewed their nation and their own loyalties. In turn, that requires an understanding of how those conceptions formed. The first chapter addresses this subject, describing the process by which the hierarchical society that emerged from the forced union of Iberian and indigenous societies served as the primary basis for a series of political crises that led to the disasters of 1846–48. Briefly put, Spain imposed, and the indigenous peoples adapted to, a structure in which order arose not from mutually created and universally accepted principles, but from institutions that regulated political, economic, and cultural conflict. These regulatory structures helped maintain fundamentally different ways of life.

With varying degrees of acquiescence, the groups that together constituted colonial México accepted Spain's role as arbiter of their society. By removing that regulatory presence without creating an alternative structure similarly acceptable to all Mexicans, the War of Independence severely weakened the traditional restraints upon the actions of various factions within the new state. Consequently, the 1821–45 period became a time of disordered and violent transition as various alliances of liberals, conservatives, monarchists, criollos, mestizos, and indígenas sought to establish control over the nation. A quarter-century of independence had so accentuated the social, cultural, and economic chasms of colonial society that México's government was forced to devote a substantial portion of its resources to waging war upon fellow Mexicans at the same time that the national state sought to repel a foreign invasion.

The next three chapters provide a chronological review and analysis of the interplay between the Mexican state, the army, the loyal and rebellious guerrilla groups, the civilian population, and U.S. forces. Chapter two addresses these issues from General Winfield Scott's landing at Veracruz on March 9, 1847, to his entrance into Mexico City on September 14 of that year. The next chapter covers the period from the fall of the capital until the signing of the Treaty of Guadalupe Hidalgo on February 2, 1848. The final chronological segment describes and assesses the little known yet critical events that occurred from the treaty signing until the last U.S. soldiers withdrew in early September 1848. Here, issues of locality, region, ethnicity, culture, and both social and economic class blended into a complex dynamic.

The conclusion evaluates the importance of the partisan movements in the 1846–48 war. This chapter also addresses the multi-generational importance of both the ideas represented by the guerrilla movements and by the United States of America's responses to this partisan challenge. *Wars within War* breaks new ground with an analysis of the war within the context of social history.

CHAPTER ONE

THE FORMATION
OF A DIVIDED
NATION

*The recent history of México, that of the last five hundred years,
is the story of permanent confrontation between those attempting
to direct the country towards the path of Western civilization
and those, rooted in Mesoamerican ways of life, who resist.*

GUILLERMO BONFIL BATALLA

The source of the divisions that so weakened México during the war with
the United States lay deep within the past. Their cultural and demographic roots originated during the Spanish conquest. Those conquerors
never became a numerical majority in the land they called Nueva España.
Hernán Cortés and the few hundred Spaniards who invaded central
México in 1519 entered a territory then populated by an estimated
18,300,000 people.[1] Even after the savageries of the conquest and the
ravages of disease, the colonists and their descendants remained a minority.
Three centuries after the first encounter between the two civilizations,
1810 census figures showed that the indigenous (*indígena*) people comprised 60 percent of México's population with the remaining inhabitants
classified as *mestizos* (22 percent) or white (18 percent).[2]

Initially, the indigenous population proved so numerous that the
Spanish succeeded in destroying central México's dominant state, the

Aztec Empire, only after establishing alliances with rival indigenous groups, who also sought the destruction of that polity. Once that particular conquest stood completed, the most immediate and important task of the new rulers consisted of defining the relationship between themselves and their far more numerous indigenous allies.

Unlike their North American counterparts, the Mexican tribes possessed centuries of experience functioning in both urban environments and in settled agricultural communities. Writing admiringly of their capacities, Cortés told his king, "I will say only that these people live almost like those in Spain and in as much harmony and order as there, and . . . it is truly remarkable to see what they have achieved in all things."[3] The Spanish considered the indigenous peoples an essential component of the colony's economic life. The manner in which they would be governed posed an interesting question and a considerable challenge for the colonists.

The Spanish first replaced the administrative superstructure of the Aztec Empire with their own, leaving intact the indigenous jurisdictions from the level of *tlatoani* (county) downward.[4] These pre-conquest structures served as the basis of the succeeding jurisdiction, the *cabecera*. Consequently, the native peoples retained some of their territory as well as a measure of economic and cultural autonomy within a colony structured as a subservient component of a major European empire.

While the Spanish authorities initially demanded tribute and forced labor from the cabeceras, the colonists subsequently sought to extend their control over remaining lands that the original inhabitants deemed their own.[5] That effort to deprive many indigenous communities of the space that formed the basis of their society severely exacerbated relations between the conquerors and conquered. Also, the Spanish concept of property as being owned by individuals could not be reconciled with the communal control of property that was the hallmark of the indigenous village.

Ownership of the land proved to be one source of tension between the westernized and criollo minority and the uneasy indígena communities. Of the other concepts that reinforced divisions within colonial society, none proved more disastrous to the future course of México than did the racial and caste prejudices embodied in the concept of *limpieza de sangre*. Literally translated, this phrase means "cleanliness of the blood." In Spain, to be of clean blood first meant that one possessed no Muslim or Jewish antecedents. However, during the fifteenth and sixteenth centuries, the definition of impurity expanded to include other groups that did not belong to what the Spanish deemed the core and corps of civilized nations. Initially, some colonists thought the indigenous inhabitants were so inferior that the question of whether or not they possessed souls remained a subject of dispute among them.

At a debate in Valladolid, Spain, in 1550, Juan Ginés de Sepúlveda set forth the position of many of the colonists. Deeming the indígenas to be "as children are to adults," he concluded that they were "little men in whom you will scarcely find even vestiges of humanity."[6] Consequently, Sepúlveda argued that they "require, by their own nature and their own interests, to be placed under the authority of civilized and virtuous princes or nations."[7] By deeming the indigenous Mexicans less than fully human, such Spaniards produced a rationale for their past and anticipated seizure of native land, for the degradation of indígenas in the forced labor gangs known as *encomiendas*, and for the "indiscriminate slaughter" and "reign of terror" described by Father Bartolomé de las Casas in his history of the Spanish conquests.[8]

To Sepúlveda's dismay, the royal government's subsequent actions brought these subjects under the crown's protection and thereby drastically reduced the colonists' control over the colony's primary labor force. Moreover, by extending royal protection to both the indigenous villages and their inhabitants, the crown ensured that the tribes retained a physical as well as a legal space of their own. The continued survival of a distinctly Mesoamerican culture within legally protected villages proved crucial to retaining their identity.

During the sixteenth, seventeenth, and eighteenth centuries, Spanish institutions regulated the economic, social, political, and religious life of the colony. Although colonists frequently tried to evade some laws, both they and the indigenous peoples accepted the legitimacy of their rulers.[9] But starting in 1759, Spain sought to alter the existing relationship. When King Charles III ascended the throne and began a series of changes known as the Bourbon Reforms. While his policies economically strengthened both Spain and her colonies, they also imposed additional regulations and taxes, and, most critically, placed Spaniards in many high offices formerly held by criollos.

The colonists responded to these events by intensifying a patriotism based upon Mexican rather than Spanish institutions. This included not only the worship of the Virgen de Guadalupe and the consequent diminution of devotion to the more Spanish Virgen de los Remedios, but the exaltation of the Mexican land and the Mexican past. The works of Agustin de Vetancourt and of the visiting Prussian scientist Alexander von Humboldt served as manifestos glorifying the vastness of Mexican territory and the enormous beauty and potential of México as opposed to Europe. Thus, criollos reacted to the limitations imposed upon them by Spain in the same manner as many groups throughout history: They intensified their own historical sense of identity. By the late eighteenth century, they also could point to distinctly Mexican forms of the Spanish language and of architecture.[10] So while still loyal to the crown, the criollos came to see themselves as people nonetheless distinct from the Spanish.

Colonial society contained many such distinctions of identity. The Spaniards' success in sustaining a government did not mean that they ruled a conceptually unified society. As one scholar of the period concluded, "The viceroyalty came to be a disintegrated mosaic of contrasting peoples, ethnic groups, languages, and cultures, disseminated in an extensive territory with poor communication."[11] That type of social structure can shatter in a time of grave crisis. Such a moment came with the 1808 collapse of imperial authority brought on by the French invasion of Spain. In México, criollo factions moved to fill the vacuum created by diminishing Spanish power while their royalist counterparts and the Spanish officials tried to counter such actions. The French decision to place Joseph Bonaparte upon the Spanish throne further muddied the question of criollo loyalty. In this unstable environment, the strength of those advocating greater autonomy from Spain grew. When Father Miguel Hidalgo y Costilla uttered his famous September 16, 1810, *grito de Dolores* summoning Mexicans to a war of independence, subsequent events demonstrated that this movement consisted not of a unified nationalism, but of two nationalisms. One was the more propertied and predominantly criollo elite and the other was the Mesoamerican majority.

As the rebel army moved forward, the actions of many of its members came to resemble those of an armed mob seeking vengeance against the more affluent and powerful colonists rather than the efforts of soldiers fighting for national liberation. Mexican statesman and historian Lucas Alamán described one such moment: "This pillage was more merciless than might have been expected of a foreign army. . . . All that could be heard was the pounding by which the doors were opened and the ferocious howls of the rabble when the doors gave way. . . . The women fled terrorized to the houses of neighbors, climbing along rooftops without knowing if that afternoon they had lost a father or a husband at the granary."[12]

The widespread looting and destruction of estates frightened many propertied Mexicans to the extent that several future presidents of México, such as Manuel Gómez Pedraza and Anastasio Bustamante, initially decided to take up arms against the independence movement at the side of the Spanish crown. In doing so, they demonstrated that their loyalty to an ordered society outweighed their desire for an independent nation.

Subsequently, a critical number of their fellow criollos demonstrated that their desire to maintain colonial México's social structure, and their own position in it, in turn outweighed their loyalty to the Spanish crown. The process by which the War of Independence concluded proved that point. That conflict ended not as the result of a great battle, but in a series of negotiations in which more than half of the royal army defected to the rebels. The ex-royalists' conversion came soon after they learned of the Spanish decision to restore the liberal 1812 Constitution of Cadiz. That document contained several provisions that Mexican conservatives found truly reprehensible. This constitution abolished the legal privileges (*fueros*) for military officers and for the clergy, granted full liberties to creeds other than that of the Roman Catholic Church, ended forced labor, abolished tithes, legalized a free press, and, most critically for the colonial elite, bestowed full citizenship upon indigenous Mexicans as well as mestizos.

Although the majority of Mexican delegates to the convention that drafted that particular constitution favored this extension of citizenship, many of México's most powerful citizens did not. These differing visions of society would constitute the basis of bitter and often violent disputes between liberals and conservatives that dominated Mexican history during the nineteenth and early twentieth centuries. In 1820, the majority of those who held positions of authority in the armed services, the church, and the civil service possessed no desire to devolve power to the general public. They preferred to keep the political, economic, and legal authority within the confines of the small group they deemed most competent to exercise such authority—themselves.[13]

Their vision of the new nation's government, the Plan of Iguala, reflected such preferences. This program, issued on February 21, 1821, respected the military and ecclesiastical rights of exemption, allowed some forms of forced labor to continue, and excluded the majority of the population from the political process. Its three cornerstones called for México to be led by a constitutional monarch rather than an elected executive, for criollos and those born in Spain to be treated equally, and for only one religion to be practiced. With the backing of the army, this proposal became the basis of independent México's first government. Thus, much of the colonial social structure remained in place.

The Plan of Iguala and the conservative power that sustained it cast a long shadow over the events of 1846–48. The decision to exclude a majority of Mexicans from participation in their national government and from much of the nation's economic life inhibited the development of strong and broadly based patriotic loyalties that México would so desperately need in its war with the United States. For the indígenas and many mestizos, a field or pueblo or municipio or valley, rather than the nation-state, continued to be the focus of their loyalties. For these Mexicans, the predominantly criollo group that sought their land remained an enemy. Moreover, the creation of an elitist regime intensified the already bitter distinctions of class and race that divided Mexican society.

An abiding commitment to inequality characterizes much of the legislation and public debate of this period. For example, José María Luis

Mora, a preeminent Mexican historian of that period, frankly set down the widely held belief of many of his fellow criollos in proclaiming, "The evil understanding that has produced the principle of legal equality almost always has been the source of innumerable grief and awful results among the peoples who have adopted the representative system."[14] That opinion reflected not only his judgment but also the conclusions of those who elected him to the Federal Chamber of Deputies and who read the influential journals he founded and edited. Mora clearly identified the Mexicans whom he deemed more capable and distinguished than others: "the white population."[15] For him, a clear conclusion flowed from that judgment: "[T]his group is the one to establish in all the world the notion that it is able [obligated] to form the Republic.[16]

Many foreign observers were quick to comment upon the inequities of Mexican society. U.S. ambassador Waddy Thompson concluded, "It is a very great mistake to suppose they enjoy anything like a social equality, even with the Indian population; and although there are no political distinctions; the aristocracy of color is quite as great in México as it is in this country."[17] The distribution of land reflected a similar disparity between classes and cultures. Thompson observed, "The lands of the country belong to a few large proprietors, some of whom own tracts of eighty and one hundred leagues square, with herds of sixty and eighty thousand head of cattle grazing upon them, whilst the Indian laborers upon those farms rarely have enough meat to eat."[18]

The official journal of the national government, *El diario del gobierno*, offered the following observation during one of its more conservative periods (1838): "[T]here always is an inequality of condition, of necessity, of talents, of climate, of the way of living and much else . . ." which in turn meant that "we do not exactly speak of the numerical majority . . ."

but of "citizens influential because of their honor, their services, their property, their education, their eloquence, their age, their experience, their usefulness, their acquaintances, their concept of work, their station, and their generosity."[19]

Significantly, *El diario* did not include the ethnic connotation of criollo ancestry in its characterization. For some mestizos and for even fewer indigenous Mexicans, a limited path into the higher echelons of society remained open. However, such advancement remained impossible for the majority of the population. Prejudices against public participation in national politics took concrete form in regulations regarding suffrage. During the 1820s, less than 1 percent of Mexico City's estimated population of two hundred thousand owned the property necessary to qualify as voters.[20] Since the capital contained a greater concentration of wealth than did the provinces, we reasonably may assume the percentage of citizens holding the franchise to have been even lower in the hinterlands. Most Mexicans remained observers rather than participants in the political process.[21]

Within that small group of participants, clear divisions emerged. The conservatives stood as defenders of much of the colonial heritage, including a strong and centralized national government, ecclesiastical and military *fueros,* and a state religion. They consistently opposed the extension of suffrage. One of their most famous and eloquent spokesmen, Lucas Alamán, went so far as to characterize the colonial administration as the last civilized government of México.[22]

The liberals of this era strove mightily against the conservative tide and achieved some noteworthy victories. Their success in abolishing slavery more than four decades before the same development took place in the United States remains one of their proudest accomplishments. Similarly, the Constitution of 1824 proved far more egalitarian than did the earlier

Plan of Iguala. Yet the liberals themselves stood divided. One faction, known as the *Puros*, attracted those members of the enfranchised minority who sought substantial change. They favored not only the abolition of the clerical and military fueros, but also the exclusion of both the church and the military from the nation's political life. Puros advocated a decentralized national government in which states enjoyed significant power. Perhaps most importantly, they advocated a significant expansion of suffrage. Between this faction and the conservative party stood the *Moderados*. While these moderate liberals sided with the Puros on many issues, they parted company with their colleagues over the extent to which reform should proceed. Given such fundamental divisions over the very nature of society, political violence became endemic.

This condition persisted even on the eve of war with the United States, at a time when national unity ought to have been a priority. In 1846, the state excluded all but a small minority from a voice in picking legislators. The regulations for this election established electoral districts not by geographic units, but by socio-economic class. Thus the owners of haciendas were guaranteed a certain percentage of seats, as were the army and clergy.[23] The antecedents for selecting deputies using such criteria existed in the medieval Spanish concept of representation by estates. In spite of the passage of a quarter of a century between the dawn of national independence and this election, the conservative regime of that day chose to base its concept of government upon this feudal Spanish practice.

Table 1.1 outlines the major requirements for participation in this election. A review of those stipulations confirms that no *campesino*, industrial worker, craftsperson, tradesperson, ranch hand, clerk, or mineworker would have met the requirements to enter any of the eight enumerated classes of voters. Also, few if any ranch owners earned the

TABLE 1.1
VOTING REQUIREMENTS FOR NATIONAL ELECTIONS AS PER THE 1846 REGULATIONS

Voter class	Deputies allotted	Deputies as a percent of the total	Requirements to run as a deputy	Requirements to vote for a deputy
Proprietors of land	38	23.75%	1000–2000 pesos in annual income	300–1000 pesos in annual income
Army, of which . . .	20	12.50%		
Army class 1 (5 deputies)			rank of division general	rank of lieutenant colonel or higher
Army class 2 (6 deputies)			rank of brigade general	rank of lieutenant colonel or higher
Army class 3 (9 deputies)			rank of lieutenant colonel or higher	rank of lieutenant colonel or higher
Business owners	20	12.50%	undefined payment	undefined payment
Clergy, of which . . .	20	12.50%		
Group 1 (11 deputies)			rank of bishop or higher	no reference to voting
Group 2 (9 deputies)			none specified	no reference to voting
Miners	14	8.75%	owners, lessees, and operators of mines	owners, lessees, and operators of mines
Industrial manufacturers	14	8.75%	factory ownership and undefined payment	factory ownership and undefined payment
Learned professions	14	8.75%	working as a lawyer, doctor, pharmacist, university teacher, or administrator	working as a lawyer, doctor, pharmacist, university teacher, or administrator
Magistrates	10	6.25%	supreme court certification	rank as a judge, auditor, or assessor
Public administrators	10	6.25%	candidates nominated by the *consejo de gobierno* and then chosen by the federal government	no voting permitted — selected by appointment
Total	160	100.00%		

income required for voting, let alone holding office in the class of land proprietors. By no means did the election regulations of 1846 signify a uniquely elitist point in time. Those regulations, the limited suffrage of the 1820s, the previously cited statements of Mora, the comments of *El diario del gobierno*, and the ongoing success of the army and the church in guaranteeing the continuation of their colonial privileges all point to the same conclusion: Most of the predominantly criollo minority that took control of México after independence favored a political structure that excluded the majority of Mexicans from meaningful participation in the life of the nation.

Although this had been the case during the colonial era, one crucial distinction between that time and the early national period was the changed status of pueblo lands belonging to both indigenous and mestizo communities. During the viceregal period, the crown granted protections to those communities in the form of titles to land and access to courts specifically charged with the responsibility of protecting their rights. As one of its first acts, the newly independent state abolished those courts. Legal and physical assaults against many communal properties soon began. In Oaxaca (1827), Veracruz (1836), and what would become the present-day state of Guerrero (1842), campesinos rebelled in defense of their lands.[24] But during the 1821–46 period, one struggle above all others exemplified both the dispute over land and the chasm separating indigenous México from the far smaller coalition governing the nation: the Álvarez Rebellion.[25] Because the forces in play during this particular revolt reemerged during the 1846–48 war, this struggle remains highly relevant to the later course of events.

The origins of that 1842–44 peasant uprising lay in the efforts of the owners of large estates in present-day Chiapas, Guerrero, Michoacán,

México state, and Oaxaca to enlarge their holdings by seizing communal lands. In taking this land, they sought to change the focus from subsistence farming designed to feed the resident population to commercial agriculture oriented toward distant markets. Through such a transformation of the countryside, the *hacendados* intended both to enhance the size of their holdings and to reap considerable financial rewards. Consequently, the citizens of many pueblos faced the grim alternatives of becoming employees on land that had once been theirs or abandoning the earth from which they drew their sustenance, upon which they built their homes, and to which they attached religious significance. To the campesinos, these communal holdings represented both their identity and independence. The loss of self-determination and the economic degradation inherent in such a choice virtually guaranteed a violent response.[26]

The igniting spark for the greatest of these revolts came in the form of an 1841 effort by President Antonio López de Santa Anna to consolidate the power of his conservative supporters by promulgating a new administrative jurisdiction that he would control. He intended to use Chilpancingo (in the present-day state of Guerrero) as the site of this new polity. Correctly recognizing this as an effort to strengthen the power of conservative *caudillo* Nicolas Bravo at the expense of his own authority, Bravo's liberal counterpart, Juan Álvarez, began organizing resistance. By virtue of his wartime service as a formidable general who rose from the ranks of the infantry and because of his status as a prominent hacendado, Álvarez exercised considerable influence in the south of México.

In 1842, he toured the Costa Chica, calling upon villagers to be prepared to defend their rights. A rebellion soon erupted. As proved to be the case with Father Hidalgo's revolt, matters rapidly spread beyond Álvarez's control. In the ensuing eruption, campesinos committed many acts of violence against the persons and properties of hacendados over a 60,000 square mile area.[27] After several years, centralist forces crushed the rebellion largely through the use of overwhelming force applied by troops brought in from other parts of the country. Álvarez cooperated with these efforts only after the uprising threatened his own properties. Although he stood for liberalism, he also remained a member of the minority that governed and owned much of México.

While the two Méxicos confronted each other across a gulf of wealth, power, education, class, and race, another nation bestirred itself. Fortified by a belief in its destiny and eager to add yet more territory to its personal and national patrimony, the United States of America stood ready to invade.

Pre-war map of México and Central America.

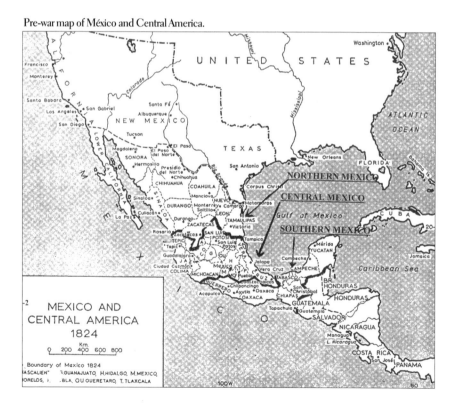

CHAPTER TWO

THE GHOSTS OF SARAGOSSA
The Invasion of Central México

It is a bad plan that admits of no modification.

PUBLILIUS SYRUS — FIRST CENTURY, B.C.

If the battles of the war between México and the United States had gone no farther than the frontiers of the two states, then the confluence of the Mexicans' civil and international conflicts never might have taken place. But that did not prove to be the case. Indeed, the plans of both governments for a war of the frontiers perished in the shooting that began on April 24, 1846.

At the start of the conflict, President James K. Polk set forth his strategy. "I gave it as my opinion that the first movement should be to march a competent force in to the Northern Provinces and seize and hold them until peace was made. In this they [the cabinet] concurred."[1] Here, Polk assumed that, by seizing some of the land he sought and then holding that territory against counter-thrusts, he would compel the other side to surrender. Implicit in this assumption was the conviction that the Mexicans would surrender approximately half of their nation while they still possessed armies in the center of the country. It is unclear by what logic the president assumed that México, which for ten years refused to acknowledge the loss of one of its states (Texas), would subsequently accept the loss of half of its national territory.

For their parts, the Mexicans clung to the hope voiced by their federal government's minister of exterior relations, Manuel de la Peña y Peña. Shortly before the outbreak of war, he informed the governors of all Mexican states: "Realistically, our only hope would not be for victory, but simply the avoidance of certain defeat. . . . At present we cannot even find the necessary funds to maintain our troops on the frontier, which is hundreds of leagues long."[2] Mexican commanders based their plans for successful resistance upon three eventualities. First, they hoped that the fighting could be confined to the frontiers. If not, they would fortify the passes of the Sierra Madre and thereby compel any sea-borne invasion force to remain on the torrid and unhealthy littoral, fighting on open plains. There, the leaders of México's army hoped that their formidable cavalry forces might cut off advancing columns of the U.S. Army. If both of these options failed, the Mexican command intended to place greater emphasis upon the hit-and-run tactics of guerrilla warfare. In that type of conflict, the highly mobile Mexican cavalry and its intimate knowledge of the home terrain would provide advantages that the more slowly moving U.S. infantry and artillery might find difficult to overcome.[3]

After the warfare north of the Rio Grande, the forces of General Zachary Taylor crossed that river and took Monterrey on August 24, 1846. This ended the Mexican government's hopes that combat could be confined to the frontier. Although the powerful Mexican cavalry force of Generals José Vicente Miñón and José Urrea continued to range across much of northern México for the duration of the war, they were incapable of destroying U.S. infantry formations and the powerful field artillery supporting the invader's columns. As of late February 1847, Taylor's forces remained firmly ensconced in

Monterrey after halting Santa Anna's advance at Buena Vista. Although they suffered many losses, Mexican forces nonetheless had avoided defeat and consequently refused to surrender.

Although both friend and foe recognized Santa Anna as a competent military leader, the combined effects of U.S. artillery and rebellious peasants frustrated the best of his efforts.
 Carlos Paris, Portrait of General Antonio López de Santa Anna, 19th Century. Museo Nacional de Historia. Reproducción Autorizada por el Instituto Nacional de Antropología e Historia.

TABLE 2.1
SUMMARY OF THE 1842 CENSUS OF MEXICO

All states		States along Scott's route to Mexico City	
Aguascalientes	69,693	México	1,389,520
Californias	33,439	Puebla	661,902
Chiapas	141,206	Veracruz	254,380
Chihuahua	147,600		
Coahuila	75,340	Total	2,305,802
Durango	162,618	% of the nation	32.86%
Guanajuato	513,606		
Jalisco	679,111		
México	1,389,520		
Michoacán	497,906		
Nuevo México	57,026		
Nuevo León	101,108		
Oaxaca	500,278	**States along or adjacent to**	
Puebla	661,902	**those on Scott's route of march**	
Querétaro	120,560		
San Luis Potosí	321,840	Guanajuato	513,606
Sinaloa	147,000	México	1,389,520
Sonora	124,000	Michoacán	497,906
Tabasco	63,580	Puebla	661,902
Tamaulipas	100,064	San Luis Potosí	321,840
Veracruz	254,380	Veracruz	254,380
Yucatán	580,948		
Zacatecas	273,575	Total	3,639,154
		% of the nation	51.87%
Total	7,016,300		

States occupied by the U.S. **in the early phase of the war**		**States occupied by Taylor**	
Californias	33,439	Coahuila	75,340
Chihuahua	147,600	Nuevo León	101,108
Coahuila	75,340	Tamaulipas	100,064
Nuevo León	101,108		
Nuevo México	57,026	Total	276,512
Tamaulipas	100,064	% of the nation	3.94%
Total	514,577		
% of the nation	7.33%		

Census data is found in foja 1, expediente 3, caja 319—1846, ramo de gobernacion, Archivo General de la Nación.

From both a political and military perspective, México's response made sense. The northern territory seized by the U.S. Army in the early phases of the war contained only a small fraction of the nation's population. As indicated by Table 2.1, the combined populations of the northern states of Alta California, Baja California, Nuevo León, Nuevo México, Chihuahua, Coahuila, and Tamaulipas totaled only 514,577, or slightly more than 7 percent of the 7,016,300 Mexicans listed in the 1842 census. Far to the south in central México lay not only the national capital and the single greatest source of government revenue (the customs house at Veracruz), but the majority of the nation's population. On either side of the invader's route from Veracruz to the national capital (Veracruz state, Puebla, and México state), lived some 2,305,802 Mexicans. Adding the populations of the adjacent states of Guanajuato, Michoacán, and San Luis Potosí increases the total to 3,639,154. That constituted a far greater population base from which to wage war than the sparsely populated northern regions of the nation. Finally, to surrender to the United States while the resources of this part of México lay untouched would have been to invite accusations of treason. So the Mexican government denied Polk the peace he sought.

Faced with such determination, the president and his advisors decided to invade central México. Given the logistical and tactical difficulties involved in a lengthy march south from its base at Monterrey to the national capital, the United States opted for an alternate plan that included the seizure of its enemy's main port of Veracruz and a subsequent march inland toward Mexico City. As the Mexican command had anticipated, the invasion would come from the nation's Caribbean littoral.

On March 9, 1847, a U.S. invasion fleet larger than any previously assembled by the navy stood off Collado Beach, two miles south of Veracruz.

Quite deliberately, General Winfield Scott and Commodore David E. Conner had chosen a landing site well beyond the range of the formidable and modern cannons of French and British origin mounted in the harbor

Scott's recognition of the political as well as the military side of the conflict was of great importance. Scott was the finest U.S. general of the era.

Minor K. Kellogg, General Winfield Scott, 1851. Oil on canvas. Collection of The New-York Historical Society.

fortress of San Juan de Ulúa. As Scott grimly noted in his memoirs, these artillery pieces "had the capacity to sink the entire United States navy."[4] In the late afternoon, the invading soldiers piled into their surfboats. By 5:30 P.M., the initial assault force of fifty-five hundred men stood on dry land. The landing took place without the loss of a single American life.

Although Scott and Conner carefully planned the landing, they did not know if the U.S. Army now would confront a fierce foe ardently supported by a civilian population eager to join in the struggle or merely a weak national army lacking popular support. If the more than 3.5 million Mexicans living in proximity to Scott's intended line of march fully participated in an intense defense of the nation, literally hundreds of thousands of able-bodied and eager volunteers would be available to fight the invader. By contrast, if the great majority of Mexicans along Scott's route proved quiescent, the U.S. Army's chance of success would be much greater.

Officers trained at the United States Military Academy learned what might be the results of such an uprising by studying the widely read works of the most famous military theorist of their day—Baron Antoine Henri Jomini. This scholar-general's experience as one of Napoleon Bonaparte's most valued military strategists and commanders included a leading role in the invasion of Spain and the subsequently disastrous efforts to pacify that nation. The brutality with which the French troops treated the civilian populace, their zealousness in assaulting widely respected social practices, and their hostility to the Catholic Church fanned the flames of resistance. Given such conduct, as well as the brutal tactics that Bonaparte employed in his struggles against Spanish guerrillas, the clergy joined patriots in converting their struggle against the invader into a broadly based nationalist uprising. Jomini described one example of the ferocity of such resistance in his account of the siege of the city of Saragossa: "Priests, monks, citizens, peasants as well as the military, were inflamed with unbounded enthusiasm. Never were so many different passions directed toward the same object. Pride, patriotism, fanaticism, national and military honor—all the most powerful motives of human action were put into play to render the defense a desperate one."[5]

In paying homage to his foes, the French general recalled, "It would require the pen of a Homer to describe the heroic scenes of this siege, where art and well-directed courage finally triumphed over the strength and energy of despair."[6] Jomini claimed that Spanish casualties at the siege of Saragossa included 15,000 soldiers and 30,000 civilians. He listed his own casualties at less than 5,000.[7] Because the army that Scott took with him to Veracruz totaled little more than 12,000 men, even one victory such as Jomini's triumph at Saragossa would have been pyrrhic. The prospect of such an outcome concerned U.S. civilian and military leaders throughout the war. The president himself became involved in the efforts to prevent a religiously based uprising.

As commander-in-chief, Polk asked a senior cleric of the church, Bishop John Hughes of New York, to assign some Spanish-speaking American priests "to visit México in advance of the army, for the purpose of giving assurance to the Catholic clergy that under our constitution, their religion and church property would be secure, and that so far from being violated, both would be protected by our army, and in this way avoid their active hostility in the pending war."[8] With satisfaction, Polk recorded the bishop's agreement with these proposals and also noted that cleric's willingness to visit the archbishop of México should the U.S. government desire him to do so.

The president by no means stood alone in his concerns about a potential mass uprising. General Zachary Taylor, who commanded the nation's forces in northern México, so dreaded the possibility of a popular uprising that he chose to battle against a far larger Mexican army at Buena Vista rather than endure the alternative of being besieged at Monterrey. The U.S. commander later argued that if such a siege had begun, "it would have been the signal for the rising of the whole country; every depot on the Rio Grande would have been at once abandoned, taken, or destroyed, all the artillery and cavalry horses and every animal belonging to the trains would have been destroyed or starved. . . ."[9]

Nine months after Taylor penned the preceding words about a popular uprising, Scott's chief of intelligence, Colonel Ethan Allen Hitchcock, grimly noted of "news received from Colonel Clark at Matamoros [in northern México] that General Worth has fallen back from Saltillo and Monterey [sic] + the Doctr [sic] adds that the people of Matamoros are more insolent than they have been + the opinion prevails that the whole country is ready to band together + an attack on Matamoros is considered probable."[10] Northern México remained hostile territory for the U.S. Army.

The Mexicans through whose territory Scott's army would pass differed from their northern counterparts in Taylor's area of operations in at least one respect: There were a lot more of them. As indicated by the 1842 census, 4,458,020 people lived in central México with 2,305,802 of them located in the three states (Veracruz, Puebla, and México) through which the U.S. Army would pass en route from the coast to the national capital. By contrast, the three northern states of Coahuila, Nuevo León, and Tamaulipas that constituted Taylor's main theater of operations contained only 276,512 Mexicans. So Scott's forces would be traveling through territory occupied by almost nine times as many people as in the north. With his army of barely 12,000 men, Scott could not have survived a furious and broadly based guerrilla movement such as that faced by Jomini. The U.S.

general-in-chief was well versed in the history of the Napoleonic Wars, and he kept more than a dozen volumes about French campaigns of that era in his library.[11]

To reduce the likelihood that the conduct of his troops would serve as a catalyst for increased guerrilla recruitments, Scott adopted several tactics. First, he took vigorous steps to prevent his troops from committing hostile acts against Mexican civilians. His General Order 87 of April 1, 1847, stipulated harsh punishment for U.S. soldiers committing crimes such as assassination, murder, rape, and malicious assault.[12] The first record of a death sentence imposed for violation of one or more of the above-cited acts occurred barely a week later. On April 9, 1847, General Order 101 stated that following his conviction on charges of rape and theft, Isaac Kirk, "a free man of color, a resident and citizen of the United States . . ." would be hanged.[13] One student of Scott's campaign concluded, "After several public whippings and a hanging, such offenses by the general-in-chief's soldiers abated in central México."[14]

Bluntly, Scott reminded his troops that their survival as an army depended upon minimizing civilian hostility. He explained, "As the season is near when the army may no longer expect to derive supplies from Vera Cruz [sic], it must begin to look exclusively to the resources of the country." Scott then pointed out that "those resources, far from being over-abundant near the line of operations, would soon fail to support both the army and the population, unless they be gathered in without waste and regularly issued by quartermasters, and commissaries." Then, he proceeded to the obvious conclusion: "[The supplies] must be paid for, or the people will withhold, conceal, or destroy them. The people, moreover, must be conciliated, soothed, or well treated by every officer and man of this army, and by all its followers.[15]

In theory, this policy would mitigate with cash and courtesy two of the great catalysts of the Spanish resistance against Bonaparte: looting and brutality. To minimize the possibility of a religiously based revolt, Scott instructed his soldiers to respect Catholic property and practice. On April 11, 1847, he issued a proclamation to all Mexicans declaring: "We are the friends of the peaceful inhabitants of the country we occupy, and the friends of your Holy Religion, its hierarchy, and its priesthood... crowded with devout Catholics, and respected by our government, laws and people."[16]

However, troops in the field frequently disregarded Scott's mandates on the treatment of the civilian population. Several factors accounted for this turn of events. First, some undisciplined soldiers did not consider themselves obligated to follow his orders. Shortly after the fall of Veracruz, Scott angrily told his subordinate commanders that in spite of his orders: "many undoubted atrocities have been committed in this neighborhood by a few worthless soldiers—both regulars and volunteers, which though stamping dishonor on the entire army, remained unpunished because the criminals have not been seized and reported by eye-witnesses of the atrocities."[17] A similar problem had plagued the U.S. commander in northern México. On February 9, 1847, General Taylor admonished his troops about the practice of, "marauding and maltreating the Mexicans."[18] This problem persisted throughout the war. As late as March 11, 1848, Colonel Thomas Childs confined his personnel to quarters for repeated offenses of drunkenness, theft, robbery, and misconduct in the city of Puebla.[19]

Although some lapses of discipline probably would occur in any large body of troops, the constancy and severity of this problem within the U.S. Army's ranks merits mention. The areas in which such conduct occurred absolutely corresponded to the rise of civilian partisan formations that henceforth made the U.S. military experience in México a miserable one. Part of the difficulty lay in the awkward situation of the volunteer regiments.

Unlike their counterparts in the regular army, soldiers who served in these units commonly elected their officers. Some of these elected commanders were unwilling to discipline their newfound constituents. Others were incapable of training their subordinates in tactics or discipline simply because they themselves had received none. The general conduct of the volunteer units prompted Lieutenant George Gordon Meade to complain, ". . .you will hear any Mexican in the street descanting on the conduct of the 'tropes de linea' as they call us, [and] the dread of the 'voluntarios.' And with reason, they have killed five or six innocent persons walking the streets, for no other reason than their own amusement; to be sure; they are always drunk and in a measure responsible for their conduct. They rob and steal the cattle of the poor farmers."[20] Meade was by no means alone in criticizing the volunteers.

After characterizing a regiment of Illinois volunteers as men "unworthy of the name of soldiers," Scott's chief of intelligence, Major Ethan Allan Hitchcock, declared, "The whole volunteer system is wholly indebted for all its reputation to the regular army without which the [illegible] body of volunteers in México would have been an undisciplined mob, incapable of acting in concert, while they would have incensed the people of México by their depredations upon persons of property."[21] The ongoing adventurism and lack of discipline within the ranks of the volunteers contributed to the aggravation of tension between the invading army and Mexican civilians. Exceptions to these harsh judgments, such as found in some of the Tennessee and Mississippi units, were far and few between.[22]

Religious prejudice constituted another source of hostility between the U.S. Army and the inhabitants. Although Scott ordered that the property and rites of the Catholic Church be respected, his command filtered down to the ranks through a corps of officers that reflected the nativist prejudices of the time. In fact, if not in name, discrimination against U.S. Catholics serving in the ranks of their nation's army remained widespread."[23] Scott's order for toleration went against the grain of prejudices that were widely held by many segments of his nation's citizenry.

The religious bigotry that the general-in-chief sought to constrain was a particularly intense sort of hatred. In the 1840s, U.S. nativist anxieties focused primarily upon Catholic immigrants. Only two years before the war began, Philadelphia was convulsed by a major riot that began over the issue of whether the Catholic (King James) or Protestant (Douay) Bible would be used in public schools. The disturbance quickly took on anti-Catholic overtones. In the prior decade, an anti-Catholic riot in Charlestown, Massachusetts, resulted in the burning of an Ursuline convent. In New York City, riots targeting Roman Catholics took place during the colonial era as well.[24]

Further difficulties arose from choices made by Scott in resolving a dilemma that confronts any army waging war on foreign soil. At one extreme, the leader of an invading force holds the option of imposing strict rules of engagement that go to extraordinary lengths to minimize civilian casualties, even at the cost of increased casualties to one's own forces. On the other end of the spectrum, we encounter the commander who conducts his campaign with little or no regard for non-combatant casualties. Although Scott placed a high priority upon not provoking the sort of resistance that confounded Napoleon's forces in Spain, he nonetheless opened his campaign in central México by taking Veracruz with tactics that produced civilian casualties far higher than should have been the case.

Throughout the nineteenth and twentieth centures, this principal port of Mexico marked the start of any
invader's route to the national's capital.
Artist unknown, Perspective of the port of Veracruz, 19th Century. Archivo General de la Nación.

As noted earlier, Scott realized that a direct assault on Veracruz's
harbor castle of San Juan de Ulúa would result in the destruction of
Commodore Conner's fleet. Consequently, he devised a more indirect
route to take both that fort and the city itself. First, he ordered his troops to
march north from Collado Beach and begin constructing a semicircular
siege line around the city. Behind that barrier, Scott positioned both his
largest cannons as well as even larger caliber artillery loaned by the U.S.
Navy for the duration of the battle. In his memoirs, the general explained
that because the "impregnable" castle did not have an ample supply of
food and water, he intended to force its surrender by starving the garrison
into submission. To accomplish that objective, he needed only to capture
the city that was the source of the fort's supplies.[25]

Following the refusal of the governor and commander-in-chief of the
port to surrender, Scott ordered the bombardment of Veracruz. During
the ensuing fifteen-day siege, "our army had thrown 3,000 ten inch shells,
200 howitzer shells, 1,000 paixhun shot, and 2,500 round shot on the

whole weighing about half a million pounds! Most effective and most terrible was the disaster and destruction they caused within the walls of the city, whose ruins and whose mourning attested both the energy and the sadness of war."[26] The bombardment was so severe that the British, French, and Spanish consuls sent a letter to Scott on March 24, 1847, asking for a truce to "enable their respective compatriots to leave the place with their women and children as well as the Mexican women and children."[27] The U.S. commander denied these requests and stated that a suspension of hostilities would be granted only if the request for the cease-fire was "accompanied by a distinct proposition of surrender."[28] The bombardment continued. Three days later the city surrendered. A Mexican summary of the damage done by the bombardment listed Veracruz's losses at 350 dead soldiers, 400 dead civilians, 250 persons injured, and five million pesos of property damaged.[29] This same observer's estimate of the total weight of shot fired into the city (464,460) pounds actually is somewhat less than Scott's figure.[30]

A participant in the siege, Lieutenant John James Peck, wrote, "The city is much injured and it will be some time before they can repair the damage. Our shells were very destructive. Hundreds of poor women and children have been killed or injured for the maintenance of Mexican honor, while soldiers were safe in the bomb proofs or comparatively so near the wall."[31] Another U.S. officer present at the siege, Robert Anderson, wrote, "It really goes to my heart to be compelled to do my duty when I know that every shot either injures or seriously distresses the poor inoffensive women and children, who have neither part nor lot in the war."[32] Jacob Oswandel, a soldier in the line during this siege, graphically noted, "To-night, I was put on picket-guard, stationed near the walls of the doomed city, and I could plainly hear the people cry out for the *rendiren tregar de ciudad* [surrender the city] before they were all killed off. That these Yankees won't give up firing."[33]

Subsequently, Scott denied that his bombardment wrought such damage, arguing, "The enemy's loss in killed and wounded was not considerable, and of other persons-citizens — not three were slain — all being in stone houses, and most of the inhabitants taking refuge in basements."[34] This assertion requires one to believe that the net result of close to half-a-million pounds of ammunition fired into a compact city resulted in only three civilian casualties. In his memoirs, Scott also argued that to postpone the bombardment would have exposed his troops to both yellow fever and to Mexican troops then forming behind him to attack and end the siege.[35] His assertion that the imminence of the fever required him to act at once rests on the assumption that a truce of even one day might have had dire consequences for the health of his troops. In reality, Scott's columns did not march westward from Veracruz toward Mexico City until April 19, a full three weeks after the surrender of the city.

Also, the general-in-chief subsequently contradicted his own argument that he needed to take Veracruz as rapidly as possible to forestall a Mexican attack upon his besieging army. Specifically, he later wrote that Santa Anna "had returned to his capital, and was busy collecting additional troops, mostly old, from every quarter of the republic, in order to crush the invasion, should it advance, at the first formidable pass in the interior."[36] Thus, Scott at one point argued that the Mexicans intended to block his advance at a point some distance from Veracruz (Cerro Gordo) and then at another time asserted that the Mexicans intended to attack his army as they besieged the city.

Scott's refusal to allow a one-day truce to evacuate civilians reflects his willingness to accept a higher civilian death toll rather than suffer even a slight delay in his own plans. That decision remains the choice of every besieger. However, an invader who wishes to cultivate the best of relations with a civilian populace should not expect to do so after refusing to grant non-combatants twenty-four hours to leave a city under heavy and intense bombardment. In Veracruz, Scott's disregard for civilian casualties mirrored his previous work as commander of the 1838 expulsion of the Cherokee nation from Georgia. They offered no violent resistance, but en route, 4,000 out of a total of 13,000 exiles died.[37] Scott conducted the operation with scant consideration for civilian casualties.

To these problems must be added the fresh and bitter legacy of the behavior of both Mexican and U.S. forces in the earlier warfare in northern México. In summarizing the situation, General Taylor wrote, "I deeply regret to report that many of the twelve months' volunteers in their route hence of the lower Rio Grande have committed extensive depredation [sic] and outrages upon the peaceful inhabitants. . . . Were it possible to rouse the Mexican people to resistance, no more effectual plan could be devised than the very one pursued by some of our volunteer regiments."[38]

Although Taylor's comments focused upon the volunteer regiments in northern México, reports of such conduct also extended to his mounted anti-guerrilla force, the Texas Rangers. A U.S. soldier who served in this area concluded, "Between the Rangers and the guerrillas, the unfortunate inhabitants of the states of Nuevo León and Tamaulipas had a hard time of it during the summer of 1847. Plundered by both sides, their lives often taken, and their wives and daughters outraged and carried off, they realized fully how terrible war is."[39] These events in the Mexican provinces bordering Texas during the first year of the conflict resulted in an escalating cycle of reprisal and counter-reprisal. This pattern would be repeated as the main theater of war subsequently shifted a hundred miles south to central México between Veracruz and Mexico City.

In response to guerrilla attacks, Scott put into practice a policy of collective punishment similar to that first tried in the far north. As implemented by Taylor, this tactic required Mexican civilians to pay for damages that partisans inflicted upon U.S. supplies.[40] Scott altered Taylor's policy of imposing fines upon entire communities by instead placing such liability only upon the mayors of those towns. Those Mexicans officials who wished to avoid such a penalty could do so only by detecting and then punishing their compatriots who attacked the U.S. forces.[41] This policy assumed that the mayors possessed the military skills and resources necessary to pursue and destroy partisan formations. There is no record of Mexican mayors having done either.[42] However, the threat to deprive these officials of their property well might have diminished any urges to counsel restraint and cooperation with fellow Mexicans.

Also, the U.S. command injected a less prominent but nonetheless noteworthy irritant into its relationship with the civilian population by the choice of some of its allies. In particular, the recruitment of the despised Manuel Domínguez, who served with U.S. troops in many missions as leader of the Mexican Spy Company, alienated local citizens. On April 20, 1847, General William Worth recruited Domínguez, a man regarded by several prominent citizens of the city of Xalapa as "a noted and dangerous robber."[43] Worth enlisted his services with these words: "You have been pointed out to me by your enemies in this city as a dangerous man. You are called an enemy by the Mexicans and treated as an enemy and feared as one. What is to prevent you from serving us? We want your knowledge of the country and we know you are a brave and daring man."[44]

Domínguez's first five compatriots joined him after Worth secured pardons releasing them from prison. A Maryland volunteer described the fully assembled company as "composed of the worst-looking scoundrels I ever saw. Robbers and banditti before the war, their characters were not improved (by it)."[45] The headquarters of the army subsequently held these particular Mexican allies in such low esteem that on October 17, 1847, its staff issued the following pass to their commander: "The bearer of this note (Domínguez) with the Native Spy Company, is on his way to Vera Cruz [sic] with dispatches for the headquarters of the U.S. Army. . . . Commanding officers of stations or of troops, in march, are desired to treat the party with kindness (so long as they continue to deserve it) and give them any facilities that may be necessary to enable them to better accomplish that mission."[46] Thus, the inhabitants of central México received a combination of measures harsh and subtle as well as cruel and conciliatory during part of 1847.

Although partisan attacks upon the invader never assumed the proportions, the ferocity, or the religious fervor of Spain's hostility to the French invaders, guerrillas emerged as a major factor for both governments between 1846 and 1848. The most amply documented partisan group began as an auxiliary force of the Mexican army created in the aftermath of the battle of Cerro Gordo, April 17–18, 1847. At that fateful site, the U.S. Army sought to storm the pass that divided the torrid littoral plain of coastal México from the higher ground leading to the national capital. In describing the outcome, a noted Mexican historian wrote, "Our reverse at Cerro Gordo was a rout as complete as it was shameful. Everything was lost."[47] That battle indeed did mark a nadir. The rout proved so complete that six days later, the defeated army abandoned the fortress of Perote, leaving fifty-four cannons in good working order for the advancing enemy.[48] Officers did not even bother with the simple and brief procedure of spiking the artillery.[49] However, other Mexicans proved far more resolute.

Ten days after the events at Cerro Gordo, on April 28, 1847, Pedro María Anaya, substitute president, decided to capitalize upon willingness to resist the invader by signing a decree calling for the establishment of a

In the aftermath of the defeat at Cerro Gordo, Anaya possessed the fortitude and presence of mind to summon into being the Light Corps, partisans of Mexico.

A. Nunez, Portrait of General Pedro Mariá Anaya, 19th Century. Museo Nacional de las Intervenciones. Reproducción Autorizada por el Instituto Nacional de Antropología e Historia.

light corps to function as part of the national guard.[50] This document stated that units of this exclusively volunteer force could be raised "by any citizen having sufficient means and influence in the country in which he resides" as soon as those Mexicans who wished to do so received the federal or state government's authorization [*patente*] to proceed.[51] As an additional incentive, the national government promised to reimburse any commanders for the expense of funding the operations of their own units. In addition to assisting the armed forces, the light corps had received the task of apprehending *malhechores*, [evildoers]. Also federal stipulations mandated that the holder of each federal grant recruit at least fifty men, create a command structure including junior and non-commissioned officers, keep diaries of operations, and confine his activities to a geographic area defined by the government. This *reglamento* constituted a call to partisan warfare.

In restricting the qualifications for a patente to those with "means and influence," the regime in Mexico City provided a clear demonstration of its enduring elitist mentality. Because only a very small minority of Mexicans possessed such wealth and influence, these requirements excluded all but a few from qualifying for such an appointment. In submitting a proposed budget for a mounted partisan force of 200 men, military surgeon Santiago Humphrey demonstrated the extraordinary level of wealth required to equip a guerrilla group.[52] Table 2.2 summarizes Humphrey's costs to outfit and recruit a 200-man unit—24,570 pesos, a figure that included no provision for additional food, forage, or ammunition once the soldiers exhausted their initial supplies. Even that start-up budget totaled roughly four times the annual salary of a federal cabinet minister; therefore, this reglamento clearly demonstrates the government's preference for placing partisan groups under the command of only the most affluent and loyal of the nation's citizens.[53] In this regard, the policy of the national government

TABLE 2.2

SANTIAGO HUMPHREY'S PROPOSED BUDGET FOR A PARTISAN GROUP OF 200 MEN

Quantity	Item	Cost per unit in pesos	Total cost in pesos
200	horses	25	5,000
200	harnesses	12	2,400
200	blankets	4	800
200	hats	4	800
200	rifles	20	4,000
400	pistols	6	2,400
200	swords	6	1,200
200	sets of clothes	13	2,600
200	pairs of shoes	2	400
400	spurs	1	400
6	cargo mules	40	240
200	powder flasks	2	400
200	cartridge bags	2	400
400	pounds of powder	2	800
200	illegible	0.5	100
200	enlistment bonuses	12	2,400
1	start-up supplies	1	200
2	bugles	15	30
Total			24,570

very much resembled those of the Spanish kings during the reconquest: Commissions to lead belonged to those who already led.

Seventy individuals received authorization to organize such corps. Table 2.3 lists names, titles, and authorized areas of operation. Some of these commanders raised forces that presented a considerable challenge to the U.S. Army; others made no recorded contribution to the war effort. When these men received their patentes, the Mexican government and

TABLE 2.3
RECIPIENTS OF PATENTES FOR LIGHT CORPS OPERATIONS

Commander	Honorofic	State(s) in which the authorized area of operation is located	Area of authorized operation
_____ Francisco, Miguel	Colonel	México	Actopán and Zaculatipán
Alamán, Domingo	Captain	Jalisco	Tequila, San Blas
Alamán, Juan	Don	México	Texcoco
Alamán, Miguel	Don	Guanajuato	Grafruato
Anaya, Cirilio Gomez de	General	not specified	Cauton del Lago Sur
Anaya, Crispo Gomez	General	not specified	Ciudad de Lagos
Arechega, José Maria	Colonel	Federal District	Federal District
Asunsolo, Juan Manuel	Colonel	Durango	none listed
Baigon, Miguel	none	México	Cuexayabaya
Berasa, Mariano de	Comandante	not specified	none listed
Buisenos, Julio Miguel	none	Veracruz and México	none listed
Burgos, José Cipriano	none	México	Xuichitepec
Carmona, Angel	Lt. Colonel	México	none listed
Carrera, Rafael	Don	San Luis Potosí	Hacienda de Carro
Castro, Cirilio	Don	Federal District	Federal District
Celada, Juan José Rodriguez	none	not specified	none listed
Cortes, Felipe Neri	Don	Veracruz	Tantujuea and Ozuluama
Costina, José Gomez de	General	México	Hahuilipan and Tlalcopan
Dorantes, Manuel	Don	Guanajuato	San Felipe and Huatlamoca
Entrechego, José Maria	Colonel	Federal District	Federal District
Ezeta, Luis	none	México	Tlalpan
Falcon, Manuel	none	Guanajuato	San Cristobál, Tlahuapantla, et al.
Fernand, Miguel	Lt. Colonel	México	Tluihalpan
Flores, Ignacio	none	Nuevo León, Tamaulipas, and Coahuila	none listed
Flores, Ygnacio	none	Nuevo León, Coahuila, and Tamaulipas	none listed
Galán, Norvento	Don	Nuevo León and Tamaulipas	none listed
Geirrero, Guillermo	Don	Guanajuato	Guanajuato
Gonzales, Ganio	none	México	Toluca
Gonzales, Plutarco	none	México	Toluca
Gonzales, Ricardo	Don	México	Texcoco
Gutmantz, Simon	none	not specified	none listed
Iturbide, Saba	Don	Puebla	none listed
Jarauta, Celedonio de	Presbyterio	Noreste	none listed
Jimenez, José Maria	Colonel of Cavalry	Tlaxcala	none listed

Continued next page

TABLE 2.3 *Continued*

Commander	Honorofic	State(s) in which the authorized area of operation is located	Area of authorized operation
Llorente, Anastasio	Captain	Veracruz	Tuxpan
Marroqui, Joaquin	Don	Hidalgo	Pachuca
Matamoros, Felix	none	Morelos	Cuernavaca y Cuatla
Mendez, Elutherio	Colonel	México	Chalco y Coyoacan
Moinafuentes, Juan Maria	Don	Tamaulipas	Tula y Jilotepec
Montano, Manuel	Don	Michoacán	Llanos de Apan
Nasadro, José Ignacio	General	Puebla and México	none listed
Nunez, Gabriel	Colonel	Veracruz	none listed
Obregon, Pablo	none	México	Cuautillan
Olanez, Miguel Hernandez	none	México	Huichapan
Osbe, Miguel	Cura	México	Tulaningo
Peza, Juan Nepomucino	Lt. Colonel	México	Cuautitlán y Tula
Ponce de León, Mariano Paredes	Captain	not specified	none listed
Ramo, Francisco	none	México	Actopán, Pachuca, Real de Monte
Rayon, Antonio	none	not specified	Ciudad Morelos
Rivera, Mariano	Don	México	Toluca
Rivera, Pablo	Don	Norte y Oriente (two multi-state fronts)	none listed
Rorar, (Boras ?) Vicente	none	Federal District	Federal District
Rosa, Miguel Vicente	Don	Federal District	Federal District
Rosas, Vicente	Don	Noreste	none listed
Ruisenor, Miguel	none	Veracruz	Tampico and Veracruz
Sabedra, Francisco	Don	Huasteca	none listed
Salas, Mariano	General	Federal District	Federal District
Soto, Ignacio y	Don	México	Chalco
Talavia, Ignacio	Don	not specified	none listed
Temimilpa, Miguel	Don	not specified	none listed
Teran, Francisco	Don	Veracruz	Tlalcotalpán
Terreros y Villarin, Pedro Romero de	Don	México	Tiraguea
Tesseson, Manuel	Don	México	Hacienda de Jalpa
Tlessan, Domingo	Captain de Cab.	Jalisco	Tequila, San Blas
Torre, Miguel Joaquin de la	Don	Noreste	none listed
Vega, Felipe de la	Don	Querétaro	Vemacacion de Tequiquepan
Villavicencio, José Nunez	Don	México	none listed
Vuda, José Maria	Lt. Colonel	Federal District	Texcoco
Zalasar, Pedro	Capitan	not specified	none listed
Zandenate, Francisco	Don	Guanajuato	Guanajuato

Applications and authorization for patentes are found in fojas 2505, 2582, and 2586 Expediente XI/481.3 of the Archivo de la Defensa Nacional, Mexico City, D.F.

its agents deemed them loyal leaders. As time passed, some of them, in particular Padre Celedonio de Jarauta, rose against the national government in armed rebellion.[54]

The list of Mexicans who received light corps commissions is noteworthy not only for the names on it, but also for the names that are absent. As indicated in Table 2.4, no citizen of the states of Aguascalientes,

TABLE 2.4

PATENTES ISSUED IN RELATION TO POPULATION

State	Population	Population as a percentage of the nation	Patentes issued	Patentes as a Percentage of the total	Notes
					1
Aguascalientes	69,693	0.99%	0	0.00%	
Californias	33,439	0.48%	0	0.00%	2
Chiapas	141,206	2.01%	0	0.00%	
Chihuahua	147,600	2.10%	1	1.30%	
Coahuila	75,340	1.07%	1	1.30%	
Durango	162,618	2.32%	1	1.30%	
Guanajuato	513,606	7.32%	4	5.19%	
Jalisco	679,111	9.68%	2	2.60%	
México	1,389,520	19.80%	29	37.66%	3
Michoacán	497,906	7.10%	1	1.30%	
Nuevo León	101,108	1.44%	3	3.90%	
Nuevo México	57,026	0.81%	0	0.00%	
Oaxaca	500,278	7.13%	0	0.00%	
Puebla	661,902	9.43%	2	2.60%	
Querétaro	120,560	1.72%	2	2.60%	
San Luis Potosí	321,840	4.59%	1	1.30%	
Sinaloa	147,000	2.10%	1	1.30%	
Sonora	124,000	1.77%	1	1.30%	
Tabasco	63,580	0.91%	0	0.00%	
Tamaulipas	100,064	1.43%	4	5.19%	
Veracruz	254,380	3.63%	6	7.79%	
Yucatán	580,948	8.28%	0	0.00%	
Zacatecas	273,575	3.90%	0	0.00%	
TOTAL	7,016,300				4

1 In cases in which a patente authorized operations in more than one state, that patente is counted in the total for each state in which the particular patente was valid.

2 Since guerilla warfare in the Californias took place under Antonio Mejares, an officer dispatched by the army for that purpose, I draw no conclusion from the California data.

3 The statistics for the state of México incorporate both population and patente data for the Federal District.

4 Census data is found in foja 1, expediente 3, caja 319 - 1846, Ramo de Gobernación, Archivo General de la Nación.

Chiapas, Oaxaca, Tabasco, the Yucatán, or Zacatecas received a patente. The absence of any citizen from these six states reflects the enduring conflict of regional with national loyalties. By contrast, almost half (45.45 percent) of all grants to organize partisan forces went to Mexicans residing in the states of Veracruz and México, which included less than a quarter (23.43 percent) of the nation's population. Here, the presence of the invader's volunteer regiments constituted a significant recruiting incentive.

Anaya and his military commanders wanted these partisan groups to wage a mobile type of warfare that would strike at one of their foe's weakest points: the supply lines along which vital munitions, money, and reinforcements moved west to Scott's main army. Also, this strategy placed primary emphasis upon the skills of the best soldiers in México's armed forces—the cavalry. Indeed, Captain Jack Hays, one of the commanders of the formidable and feared Texas Ranger detachments fighting with Scott's army, deemed the horsemanship of the enemy lancers on an open plain to be superior to that of his own men.[55] In forming the light corps, Anaya acknowledged the necessity of modifying the original plans for resisting the invaders. Having failed to hold the enemy at the frontiers or confine the invader to the coastal plain, the Mexican government would now wage guerrilla war in central México.

CHAPTER THREE

SUCCESS, FRUSTRATING SUCCESS

Cheer up, the worst is yet to come.

PHILANDER CHASE JOHNSON

Scott fully understood the danger of his position. Even if his army succeeded in procuring food and other staples from the surrounding countryside, everything else had to pass along the road from Veracruz—the replacements for soldiers whose terms of enlistment expired; the reinforcements to maintain and then to expand the size of his force; the cartridges, shells, and powder for his weapons; and the money to fund his operations. He acknowledged the "danger of having our [supply] trains cut and destroyed by the exasperated rancheros, whose houses are thinly scattered over a wide surface, and whom it is almost impossible, with our small cavalry force, to pursue and to punish." Given that menace, he faced "the consequent necessity of escorting trains seventy odd miles up, and the same down, with a meager cavalry that must from day to day become, from that intolerable service, more and more meager."[1]

Barely two months after Scott penned those words in April 1847, the partisans had developed into a force so formidable that the task of escorting a single major general, John Anthony Quitman, from the forward lines

back to Veracruz proved beyond U.S. capabilities. Scott ruefully acknowledged to Secretary of War William Learned Marcy that "at that time, (end
of May and beginning of June), it was impossible to send Major General
Quitman in safety to his new division, (understood to be on the Rio
Grande frontier) inasmuch as 1,200 or 1,500 men would have been necessary to escort him, and I have not had the means of sending a detachment
down to Vera Cruz [sic] since that time."[2]

U.S. Army records detailed continuing light corps attacks during that
month. On June 4, 1847, a supply convoy under the command of
Lieutenant Colonel James S. McIntosh left Veracruz with 128 wagons and
688 men. The partisans attacked this convoy three times on June 6. On the
following day, McIntosh halted the column at Paso de Ovejas and requested
reinforcements, having lost twenty-four wagons (12 percent of the total)
and having taken twenty-five casualties. When 500 reinforcements
arrived on June 11 under the command of Brigadier General George
Cadwaladar, the convoy's soldiers successfully attacked the National
Bridge at a cost of thirty-two dead and wounded. They then proceeded
to La Hoya, where the guerrillas attacked them on June 20 with a force
that Cadwaladar estimated to consist of 700 men.[3] A Mexican account of
the same attack also notes the loss of twenty-four U.S. wagons. However,
this record cited additional U.S. losses of 417 cargo mules and 114
[mule] carts.[4] A third account confirms these additional losses.[5] The
original escort and the reinforcements for this particular convoy totaled
1,188 soldiers, which was very close to the estimate of 1,200 given by
Scott in his explanation to Marcy.[6]

In July 1847, another supply convoy departed Veracruz with a far larger
escort than its predecessor. Led by General (and subsequently President)
Franklin Pierce, this train included 2,500 troops, 100 wagons, 700 mules,

and $1 million in specie. Some 1,400 Mexicans attacked this convoy at the National Bridge, killing thirty U.S. soldiers. Pierce then returned to Veracruz for artillery and additional troops and then set out for Puebla. During the same month, a Mexican military officer's summary of the battle claimed that the light corps killed an additional sixty soldiers in various actions between Santa Fe and Paso de Ovejas.[7] These attacks took place in spite of the fact that some partisan units found their scope of action limited by shortages of materiel. For example, toward the end of July 1847, the Santa Fe–Paso de Ovejas command reported that it had exhausted all of its supplies and that the morale of its troops suffered as a consequence.[8]

On July 12, 1847, partisans also attacked a U.S. column at the Ules River near the village of Huejutla (de Reyes) in northeast Hidalgo. In this confrontation, 550 members of the national militia ambushed a column and forced it to retreat. Although Lieutenant Colonel José María Mata did not state the size of the U.S. force he attacked, he reported that his militia captured sixty loaded mules and twenty riding horses. The light corps continued its attacks during the following month.

On August 6, 1847, a U.S. force of 1,000 men under the command of Major Folliott T. Lally set out from Veracruz. They beat back an attack at Paso de Ovejas on August 10, with eleven casualties. On August 12, this convoy fought another engagement with the Mexicans at the National Bridge. Here, Lally's troops suffered an additional fifty-one casualties and then pressed forward toward Xalapa. Total casualties for this convoy amounted to 105 men.[9] On August 13, 1847, a force of three companies (which would have been 240 men at full strength) left Veracruz to reinforce Lally's command. When this group reached the National Bridge, the Mexicans forced them to retreat after capturing every supply wagon but one.[10] To repel Lally's reinforcements, the guerrillas resorted to a weapon not usually employed by partisans: artillery. They also shot the convoy's mules, thereby rendering it impossible to remove the cargo.[11]

On August 21, 1847, reliable reports claimed that the Mexicans inflicted an additional 100 casualties on Lally's force in the vicinity of Xalapa.[12] Guerrilla formations also attacked fixed posts established by Scott's soldiers along the Veracruz–Mexico City route. During that same month, partisans operating near the Pueblan town of Guadalupe stole some wagon teams from a U.S. Army mule yard. When the owners of the animals pursued the Mexicans, the raiders withdrew at a measured pace. At some distance from the post, 300 Mexican lancers launched a charge from well-hidden positions on their pursuers' flank. More than a dozen U.S. soldiers died in the encounter.[13]

In September 1847, yet another U.S. convoy moved eastward from Veracruz. By this point, the estimations of the light corps' fighting ability was so high that Major William Booth Taliaferro observed, "The last command which left the seaboard was defeated and had to retreat . . . and we left with the full expectation of a bloody and severe fight every day until we succeeded in our enterprise, and no day broke over our heads on the march but was looked upon as the last by many of our numbers."[14]

On this particular occasion, the U.S. Army forced a passage at the National Bridge using the same tactic in formal battles—overwhelming artillery superiority. As was often the case, the advantage of heavier weaponry turned the tide. Taliaferro described the encounter: "Our shells burst all over them, and we could see them leave the fort but crouching so that we could not tell their numbers. . . . That was all, we gained the celebrated pass without a shot being fired except from the artillery and the few fired by men upon the enemy in our rear, and do not even know what was the number we drove away."[15] However, neither capturing a fortified position nor the end of daylight signaled a pause in the partisans' activities. Taliaferro ruefully observed, "Indeed it is so common to hear the reports of escopettes [shotguns] that I hardly care to get up at night to go out and see where they are fired from, and sleep soundly although I may be called to a fierce conflict before morning."[16]

The light corps remained intent on far more than nocturnal disruptions. They sought to pick off stragglers, men who otherwise became separated

A guerrilla of the Mexican Army. An antiseptically blood-free encounter between the U.S. Army and the light corps. Manuel Serrano, *Enfrentamiento de chinacos y norteamericanos*, 19th Century. Oil on Canvas, 36.5 X 49 cm. Colección Banco Nacional de México.

from their units. During the advance from Veracruz to Mexico City, General Gideon Johnson Pillow admonished his troops to avoid straggling or straying or carousing outside of camp, admitting that such actions cost his unit more casualties than did battles.[17] Perhaps the best tribute to the early effectiveness of these tactics lay in the warning Scott issued to his soldiers as they moved eastward from Xalapa on April 30, 1847: "To prevent straggling and marauding, the roll of every company of the army will be called at every halt, by, or under the eye of an officer. In camps and in quarters there must be at least three such roll calls daily. Besides, stragglers, on marches, will *certainly* [Author's emphasis] be murdered or captured by rancheros."[18]

One example of the sort of loss Scott feared had occurred several days earlier. On April 29, 1847, several parties of men belonging to the Third Illinois Regiment left their camp to forage for chicken and beef in the surrounding countryside. A party of guerrillas attacked the U.S. soldiers, killing "several." On the following day, a full company of that same regiment left to hunt both beef and guerrillas. They found no partisans. Within twenty-four hours of that company's return to camp, guerrillas killed two more of the regiment's soldiers and a member of the New York Regiment as well. All three men fell after wandering beyond the perimeter of the camp.[19]

Small parties of U.S. soldiers leaving the main body of troops on foot or on horse to perform specific missions sometimes fared no better than individual stragglers. An encounter on August 14, 1847, began when a party of dragoons led by Scott's aide de camp, Lieutenant Alexander Hamilton (descendant of the founding father), set out to determine if a foundry near Chalco could be utilized to manufacture shot and shells. A force of approximately 200 Mexican lancers surprised the dragoons, killing Hamilton and an undetermined number of others. The survey party then withdrew.[20] Similarly, when a force of eleven U.S. soldiers under the command of Captain Philip Kearney left the main column in search of sheep, partisans surprised them near San Domingo. The Americans returned to camp having lost four comrades.[21]

In addition to fighting in the field, partisans also attacked the U.S. forces garrisoned at fixed points throughout México. In the formidable central highland fortress of Perote, Colonel Thomas Claiborne complained, "The guerrillas were swarming everywhere under vigorous leaders, so that for safety the drawbridge was drawn up every night."[22] Some three hundred miles south of Perote, the U.S. garrison in the Tabascan city of Villahermosa found itself in a similar situation. Commodore Matthew C. Perry described the situation: "In the meantime, Mexican troops infiltrated the town every night to pick off Americans; this was the kind of fighting they liked and they were good at it. Commander Bigelow of *Scorpion* decided to clean up Echagaray's army at Tamulte and dispersed it; but dispersing Mexicans was no more effective than chasing hungry deer out of a vegetable garden. They always drifted back, to take pot shots at 'gringos.'"[23] The situations in which these U.S. garrisons found themselves proved to be similar to those that already had developed in northern México even before the formation of the light corps.

Some six hundred miles north of Villahermosa lay the coastal port of Tampico, Tamaulipas. There, Colonel William Gates considered the partisan threat so substantial that as early as March 27, 1847, he commanded the entire garrison to turn out under arms in the event of a fire in the town. He feared that any such blaze would be a signal for an attack.[24] To prevent partisans from using the Panuco River as an avenue for attack, Gates forbade Mexicans from landing at any points other than those regularly used for such purposes. In a final effort to secure their camp, the garrison commander terminated the employment of the local police force on the grounds that they had conspired against his forces.[25] Farther north near the Rio Grande, attacks on soldiers garrisoning the town of Camargo became so frequent that on October 14, 1846, General Gideon Pillow forbade them from leaving camp without written permission of their company commanders. He went so far as to threaten those disobeying this order with imprisonment.[26]

Interestingly, no documentary evidence exists for concluding that this state of affairs at Camargo and Tampico resulted from the actions of federally sanctioned guerrillas. To all appearances, the Mexican forces launching such attacks arose spontaneously.

Although the various partisan attacks did not overwhelm U.S. garrisons or break their supply lines, they nonetheless forced Scott to divert resources and attention to his rear. The victories that he gained against these irregular forces consisted of fighting through rather than decisively destroying the enemy formations. This partisan warfare undermined his soldiers' morale.[27] While Scott and his officers confronted the challenges posed by the Mexican army's guerrilla force, the senior leaders of México's national government simultaneously faced a threat from a wholly different group of irregular warriors.

As previously noted, an ongoing struggle between the rural indigenous peoples and peasants and the nation's elite had characterized the early national period of Mexican history. Whenever that conflict erupted into violence, the national guard or the regular army emerged as the ultimate means of force. However, the deployment of Mexican troops to face the invader's forces, and their subsequent destruction in fixed battles, gradually stripped the regime of much of its ability to repress such rural revolts. Conversely, the rebellions launched by campesinos and secessionists during the 1846–48 war often forced both the federal and state governments of México to direct some of their military forces away from the advancing invaders and toward other Mexicans. A symbiotic, if unacknowledged, relationship existed between the U.S. Army and the agrarian rebels.

The initial wave of these rebellions began in the present-day states of Colima, México, Michoacán, Oaxaca, Puebla, Tabasco, and the Yucatán. They accelerated to a level that exceeded the Mexican army's capacity to respond. The first eruption of violence occurred only one month before the war with the United States began. In March 1846, indigenous inhabitants in the district of Chilapa, México state, attacked several targets with particular force. In characterizing this situation as one part of "a war of the most barbarous nature," a Mexican federal official noted that these campesinos also sought to organize support in the adjacent area of Costa Chica.[28] Subsequently, the Mexican government dispatched a force to occupy Chilapa.

After the United States and México began fighting, agrarian-based revolts against the Mexican government erupted in many parts of the nation. On May 26, 1846, 200 *Mexiquense*[29] rebels attacked San Luis de Azoya.[30] An equal number of rebels under the command of Faustino Villalua controlled Acutumpa as of July 22, 1846.[31] These men proved willing combatants and inflicted heavy casualties upon a column of eighty government soldiers.[32]

Other guerrillas challenged federal authority in Puebla. Characterizing the source of the rebellion as indigenous pueblos, the state's governor acknowledged that, as of March 1846, he did not possess the capacity to chastise rebels in Metlatonoc and Atlamacingo.[33] Three months later, General Angel Guzman fought Pueblan guerrillas at Acatalán del Rio. On June 11, 1846, he reported taking thirteen prisoners, as well as rifles and shotguns.[34] This small victory by no means ended challenges to federal authority in the state. If the national government hoped that the revolts would be confined to these two states adjacent to the national capital, events soon proved them wrong.

One month after the clash at Acatlán del Rio, the commander of army operations, General Francisco Pacheco, wrote of "the continuous uprisings that disgracefully happen against the supreme government" in the district of Colima.[35] It is reasonable to assume that Pacheco's subsequent reference to the necessity of deploying a battalion in Colima indicates a rebellion of some consequence.[36]

During that summer of 1846, armed struggle erupted in other regions. In July, General Juan Álvarez led a force of some 3,000 men into the Oaxacan communities of Ometepec and Tecoanalpa to reassert federal sovereignty.[37] During that same month, a former and future governor of Michoacán, General José de Ugarte, fought with rebels from the pueblos of Ajuchitan and Coyuca. He reported killing seven, wounding thirty, and seizing all of their arms.[38] A further confrontation in that same state resulted in Captain Miguel Montano's forces killing fifteen rebels, taking twenty-nine prisoners and inflicting numerous casualties at the Hacienda de Santa Theresa.[39]

Although the government could claim victory in most of its encounters with rebels, such triumphs did not imply a definitive and final defeat of the rebellious pueblos by the state forces. For example, at Chilapa, the withdrawal of federal soldiers under Guzman's command resulted in so much agitation that Álvarez deemed a garrison of 150 men necessary for the maintenance of public order.[40]

The first intimations of the greatest and fiercest rebellion of indígenas since the Spanish Conquest—the Caste War—emerged in the Yucatán. That particular uprising is considered in more detail in the following chapter.

Rebellions continued in other states. In January 1847, a revolt in Tabasco accelerated to a point at which the Chiapan state government sought merely to contain the "revolution" within Tabasco's boundaries and reestablish federal control only "if possible."[41] During that same month, armed challenges in Querétaro reached a level at which that state's general command informed the national government that unspecified units destined for use against the U.S. Army could not be spared from local duties.[42] In February 1847, rebellion in the Oaxacan community of Eula caused the government to post 500 national guardsmen there.[43] In these and other instances, the task of suppressing the disorders often fell upon the state governments rather than upon the federal army. In the case of a revolt in the Pueblan village of Tepeaca, the national government's actions consisted merely of a letter from the minister of exterior and interior relations to the state governor asking that he dispatch one of his own national guard battalions to quell the rebellion.[44]

To recapitulate: During the phase of the México–United States war starting with the commencement of hostilities on April 6, 1846, and ending with the fall of the national capital on September 14, 1847, agrarian rebellions began in México state, Puebla, and in present-day Colima. Soon thereafter, revolts also erupted in Michoacán, Oaxaca, Tabasco, and Yucatán. The Mexican government confronted both an invader advancing upon the national capital and an internal foe of increasing strength. To this bloody mélange—federally sanctioned partisans, spontaneously emerging local guerrilla groups attacking U.S. forces, peasants rebelling against the Mexican government, and regular armies of the two nations fighting each other—can be added another consideration: the extent to which many Mexicans divorced themselves from the war effort.

Such attitudes emerged not as outright renunciations of allegiance, but in more subtle actions that existed in the space between mutiny or collaboration on the one hand and an unwillingness to cooperate fully in the national defense on the other. Juan Álvarez demonstrated such conduct on several occasions. For example, on April 10, 1847, he informed his superiors in the capital that his forces at Acapulco included forty-nine pieces of artillery ready for use.[45] No record of the *Archivo de la Defensa Nacional*, the *Archivo General de la Nación*, or of the National Archives and Records Administration contains any indication that Álvarez's artillery engaged in any military actions during the week between that date and April 17, 1847. Also, no document left by Álvarez or his subordinates indicates any loss or damage to these weapons during those seven days. Yet on April 17, he reported that his arsenal now consisted of a mere fifteen cannons, not of forty-nine artillery pieces.[46] There is no explanation for the apparent disappearance of thirty-three cannons. As far as Álvarez was concerned, they no longer existed for the purposes of the national government.

Then, on May 3, 1847, he even more clearly indicated his unwillingness to cooperate with the national war effort. On that day, he first respectfully acknowledged the federal government's order to move 3,000 soldiers eastward toward the capital, but then argued that the possibility of a U.S. invasion necessitated that those troops remain in Acapulco.[47] One week later, he sent a second missive, asserting that the change of climate encountered in marching from the Pacific Coast to Mexico City would prove injurious, and perhaps fatal, to the health of his men.[48] Yet in May, Mexico City's daily temperature range runs from a low of fifty-two degrees to a high of seventy-nine degrees. Those figures overlap Acapulco's similar range of seventy-two degrees to eighty-eight degrees for that same month.[49] The assertion that trained soldiers accustomed to harsh conditions could not endure a change of climate far less severe than that of a winter tourist flying home from Cancun to Chicago is indefensible. Eventually, Álvarez did march eastward, but only after receiving orders so explicit that he had no other alternative. He complied, but in a tardy and nominal manner. By doing so, he avoided a potential charge of directly disobeying an order, while at the same time denying the federal government any more than minimal support. Thus, he accomplished an important objective: conserving his own forces for future intra-Mexican conflict. His actions stand as fully consistent with the policy of a caudillo preserving an army for the use of his own cause at the expense of the nation. That "practical outlook is consistent with the factional mentality prevalent in the Mexican Army since independence."[50]

A similar attitude of reluctant, minimal, or occasionally non-existent compliance frequently appeared in other arenas. For example, in early 1847 the federal government sought to increase funds to continue the war by subjecting certain forms of church property to seizure and sale. According to the decree, the state governments were also to be part of this process. Yet on February 10, 1847, the Jaliscan legislature suspended the seizure of ecclesiastical property mandated by the national government.[51] Jaliscan politicians declared that they were not in rebellion against the regime in Mexico City. Instead, they merely rejected one manifestation of federal authority and in doing so denied additional funds to the Hacienda Ministry. Two weeks later, on February 24, the Oaxacan state government similarly refused to implement the same law.[52]

During the summer of 1847, the state of Guanajuato suspended raising cavalry and infantry forces for the national government. In a written rebuke dated July 6, 1847, the Ministry of War and Marine's *sección de operaciones* cast aspersions upon that state's rationalization that it lacked the resources to proceed with this particular effort.[53] In each of these cases, refusing to comply with a particular federal directive did not proclaim a rebellion. Rather, it indicated a different set of priorities than those of the national government.

During much of 1847, widespread apathy toward the war effort appeared. As early as May 19, 1847, the Ministry of War and Marine's operations section cited "the same indifference noted in all the Republic, particularly in the states of Tamaulipas, Nuevo León, and Coahuila." Although this report in part attributed such attitudes to the recent record of the Mexican army, the authors also noted a lack of enthusiasm for guerrilla warfare. As in the pre-war years, many Mexicans at both the upper and lower levels of society apparently divorced themselves from the greater nation and lived in *patrias chicas* (regional or state homelands).

In the south of México, such separatist movements as Chiapas' Doroteo Monterosa's gave the government much cause for concern.[54] In the nearby region of the Yucatán, Governor Miguel Barbachano y Tarrazo pleaded for federal troops to combat a separatist movement based in Campeche.[55] Although the socio-economic origins of these rebellions differed from those of the indigenously based uprisings in rural pueblos, both confirmed societal chasms so severe that not even a foreign invasion could cause Mexicans to stop fighting each other.

Even within the small group at the top of Mexican society, divisions took a severe toll upon the war effort. The most dramatic example came during the battles for Mexico City. On September 8, 1847, a U.S. force conducted a brief artillery bombardment of Molino del Rey and then launched an infantry attack. American foot soldiers faltered in the face of surprisingly strong Mexican resistance. At that moment, Álvarez and some 4,000 of his cavalry stood on the flank of the attacking force. For a brief moment it appeared as if the forces of Scott and Álvarez would confront each other on the field.

Santa Anna, who defended the capital, ordered Álvarez to charge the U.S. Army's exposed flank. He did not comply. Santa Anna concluded, "He was on the enemy flank within rifle range, and the enemy was in disorder; but just as though he had nothing to do, he sat there on his mule, playing the spectator."[56] Álvarez's decision to abstain from committing his forces to this fray weakened the Mexican army's defense of the national capital. Indeed, Santa Anna asserted that if Álvarez had ordered a charge, "the defeat of the enemy might have been complete."[57]

The factional mentality represented by Álvarez's inaction at Molino del Rey was widespread within the ranks of the army. William A. DePalo, the author of a seminal work about the Mexican army during the early national period, concluded: "At this juncture in the war, I am of the opinion that most senior Mexican military leaders viewed the war as already lost and therefore their actions were increasingly geared toward gaining political advantage in the post-war period arena. Accordingly, Álvarez was most likely unwilling to risk the military force he would need to reestablish his political authority in southern México once the war ended."[58]

But for both the invaders and the invaded, the fall of Mexico City did not signal the end of fighting.

CHAPTER FOUR

PERFECT ANARCHY

War cannot for a single minute be separated from politics.

MAO TSE-TUNG

Neither the partisan warfare waged against the U.S. Army nor the guerrilla revolts challenging the authority of the Mexican state ceased as Scott's troops entered the national capital on September 14, 1847. Instead, the events of that day only marked the end of the national army's efforts to defeat the invaders by engaging in traditional cavalry, infantry, and artillery confrontations. Partisan warfare between the two nations continued until March of 1848. Moreover, the fighting between the Mexican regime and many of its most discontented subjects did not end with the fall of Mexico City. Instead, that conflict grew in intensity and urgency. This chapter addresses the course of such events from September 14, 1847, until the signing of the Treaty of Guadalupe Hidalgo on February 2, 1848.

The fall of the national capital did not provoke a great anti-U.S. uprising among the millions of campesinos who made up the majority of Mexicans. Practitioners of warfare from Carl von Clausewitz to Mao Tse-Tung, and from Francisco "Pancho" Villa to Emiliano Zapata understood that the success of violent resistance to an occupier depended upon the active involvement of rural peasants. During the Mexican Revolution, Zapata succeeded against the coalition led by Venustiano Carranza by relying upon his loyal Morelian campesinos.[1] Villa knew that his finest units included many fighters drawn from the lower rungs of northern México's socio-economic ladder. Mao recognized that in an agriculturally based society, broad and extensive agrarian support stood as the prerequisite for any force seeking change. Even a member of the nobility such as Clausewitz deemed peasants superior to regular soldiers for waging guerrilla warfare.[2] But like its colonial predecessors and its Porfirian successors, the 1846–48 administration at Mexico City considered the lower classes good for little more than common labor.[3] During the autumn of 1847, those peasants who chose to fight most often fought against their own nation's government.

The loss of the capital and of the tens of thousands of soldiers who tried to defend the city severely weakened the ability of the national government to continue resisting the invader. Also, the loss of the port of Veracruz and the U.S. seizure of other Mexican ports along both the Caribbean and Pacific coasts denied the Mexican government its greatest single source of funding—tariffs. During the fiscal year prior to the start of the war (June 1844 to June 1845), taxes on external commerce totaled 7,033,720 pesos while all other federal taxes, including the *alcabala*, totaled only 4,161,128 pesos.[4]

Consequently, the burden of fighting the United States now fell primarily upon the light corps.[5] They continued to resist with an ardor little diminished by the loss of Mexico City. As Major John Reese Kenly ruefully noted on September 29, 1847: "If you ever saw a beehive overturned, an uncommon degree of activity moves the busy bee; imagine a half dozen hives rudely upset, and instead of bees, guerrillas were the occupants; then you can picture the buzz that was about our post from the swarms of exasperated Mexicans, who, maddened by the loss of their capital, threw themselves on Scott's communications."[6]

To the dismay of the U.S. Army, partisans promptly displayed their ability to wage unconventional warfare in urban as well as rural environments. In Mexico City, partisans took cover in houses and commercial buildings just as they had concealed themselves behind hills and in forests. Back streets and alleyways offered the same opportunity for rapid withdrawal as did foot paths in the countryside. The partisans began their urban warfare within a few hours of the Mexican army's withdrawal from Mexico City. On the very day that the U.S. commanders entered the city, Colonel Hitchcock found that a sizeable portion of the capital's civilians were by no means as ready to capitulate as their government. He vividly described the event:

The [Mexican] soldiers have left the city, but the populace is attempting what has often been threatened. Before the general [Scott] entered the city and while General Worth was leading his troops toward the plaza, Colonel Garland was badly shot from a Mexican window. The house was instantly fired upon by our artillery & since then there is firing in the streets and houses all around us. Many Mexicans [are involved] and it is easy to see that a most serious state of things may result....

5 P.M. and I rejoice that night will bring us some quiet & silence. There has been a constant firing and whizzing of balls around us all day & it is growing worse. I have been to the city council and threatened & relayed his [Scott's] order that he would destroy the city and give it to pillage if the firing did not cease. I have earnestly recommended the immediate concentration of our troops and a positive order to cease firing except in the clearest cases of self-defense.[7]

In this instance, the threat of collective punishment and the reality of close-range artillery fire subdued many of the insurrectionists. Hitchcock subsequently wrote that by 8 A.M. the following morning, the Mexican firing was negligible. However, sporadic fire continued for three more days.[8] Even one of the most prominent and stalwart defenders of U.S. conduct in this war, Justin Harvey Smith, conceded that a broad spectrum of citizens joined in the assault: "Thousands of convicts from the jail joined the populace, and in one way or another not a few of the better class cooperated. By Tornel's [federal cabinet member José María Tornel y Mendívil's] order paving stones had been taken to many of the *azoteas* [roof tops] with a view to resisting the invader step by step, and these, like very other sort of weapon, were now used."[9]

In conceding that "the populace" engaged in this collective act of resistance, Smith undermined the prevailing assumption that the events of September 14, 1847, represented nothing more than the outburst of released criminals. The veracity of that claim may be measured by the answer to a simple question: Would the first impulse of a felon just freed from jail be to throw paving stones at skirmishing soldiers backed by artillery?

Subsequently, partisans in Mexico City began using the same tactic they had previously employed in the countryside: killing U.S. soldiers walking alone or in small groups. A British volunteer in Scott's army described the effectiveness of such tactics: "When our troops first entered the city, a great number of our men fell by the knives of these miscreants, being stabbed by them when strolling intoxicated and through the low quarters of the city at night. In fact, so numerous were these street assassinations for several nights that General Scott issued an order adverting to the fact, and cautioned soldiers against leaving their quarters, unless in small parties or well-armed."[10]

That description bears a resemblance to previously cited situations occurring in Camargo during September–October 1846, in Tampico during March 1847, and on the march from Veracruz to the Valley of México. In all three locations, Mexicans targeted isolated U.S. soldiers. Some U.S. officers in Mexico City preferred to regard these attacks as isolated instances of Mexican criminals assaulting soldiers en route to or from an evening of relaxation or drinking. However, Scott's previously cited order that his men go armed and in parties, rather than singly, did not limit itself to such occasions. His admonition applied to all personnel. Justifiably, we may infer that Mexicans targeted all vulnerable troops.

Scott's order commanding soldiers in Mexico City to go armed and in groups mitigated this particular problem there. However, the problem of securing his supply lines required far more attention, as attacks against his forces persisted along the Mexico City-Veracruz route. Scott responded by taking the step that Carl von Clausewitz predicted invaders would take in such a situation: He established more fortified posts along the route of supply. One month after the fall of Mexico City, Scott declared his intention to set up a series of posts between Veracruz and Xalapa and to station a force of between 500 and 750 men at each.[11] Also, Scott decided to garrison Puebla with a force of between 1,200 and 2,000 soldiers. By November 1847, the U.S. posts at Perote, Puente Nacional, Río Frío, and San Juan consisted of 750 troops each with an additional 2,200 soldiers stationed at Puebla.[12] The 5,000 troops thus committed to anti-partisan warfare constituted 20 percent of the 24,500 U.S. soldiers in central México at that time.[13] If we add the 1,200 escorts for the supply trains to the number of soldiers stationed at these posts, then the percentage of U.S. forces involved in counter-guerrilla work rises from 20 percent to 25 percent of the total force. Clearly, the partisans fought effectively, and they certainly posed a significant threat to the U.S. Army well after the regular Mexican army ceased to offer large-scale resistance.

In an effort to destroy these foes, U.S. commanders pursued them whenever possible. Yet, on more than one occasion, the Mexicans proved themselves the more mobile force even in the face of defeat. An encounter on the night of October 18, 1847, between the force led by Brigadier General Joseph Lane and a large partisan force led by General Joaquín Rea provided one such example. This clash began when Lane's troops came under fire from the Mexicans at Atlixco, Puebla. Lane responded by posting his artillery on a hill overlooking the town and then initiated a forty-five-minute artillery bombardment that he directed toward the most populated parts of the community. Following the bombardment, he sent an advance force into Atlixco and later that evening followed up with the main body of his force. According to Lane, the Mexicans stated that their own casualties totaled 219 wounded and 319 killed. However, he conceded that Rea escaped with some of his men and several artillery pieces. Lane considered Atlixco a guerrilla base and reported, "So much terror has been impressed upon them, at thus having the war brought to their own homes, that I am inclined to believe they will give us no more trouble." As Lane conceded, Rea escaped and would fight again another day. Although the Mexicans suffered severe losses, their commander and at least some of his artillery were mobile enough to escape their pursuers.[14]

Lane's attitude toward the civilians and theirs toward him also merit mention. At Atlixco, he faced several choices. He could have surrounded the town and then waited until daylight before beginning his assault. Alternately, he had the option of minimizing damage to civilians and property by forgoing an artillery bombardment and accepting far higher casualties to his own forces in a street battle. Instead, he chose a third path that minimized his own losses while increasing those of both enemy soldiers and civilians: a substantial shelling of the community with clearly stated goals. As at Veracruz, the U.S. commander placed the highest priority upon minimizing his own casualties and achieving the most rapid possible results. While his strategy remains defensible in a strict military sense, Lane's action would not conciliate civilians to the presence of the occupier any more than did Scott's bombardment at the siege of Veracruz.

During the fall of 1847, the U.S. Army also began trying to destroy the partisans' supply and rest areas. As early as September 13, 1847, Lieutenant Colonel George Wurtz Hughes recommended that troops be sent from Veracruz to Paso de Ovejas with instructions "to destroy *all* [Author's emphasis] the Ranchos off the road, as they constitute the depots and places of resort."[15] Apparently, he deemed all owners of small plots of land in that area to be guilty of participating in or supporting the partisan attacks. Hughes put that policy into practice on the same day that he recommended it to his superiors and then enthusiastically described his own conduct: "He [Captain Heintzelman] was attacked last night by a strong party at Passo Ovejas [*sic*], but repelled it with no other loss than one man wounded. The rascals had the satisfaction of finding their house in a blaze on their return home. They were destroyed by a party of my command, who attempted to bring them action, but without effect."[16] Hughes did not provide an explanation of the means by which he determined that the destroyed home belonged to the party of guerrillas whom he had failed to apprehend, let alone identify. By no means did Hughes stand alone in practicing such tactics. In reviewing these events, even Justin H. Smith conceded, "The torch was applied with much liberality, on suspicion, and sometimes on general principles, to huts and villages; and in the end a black swath of destruction, leagues in width, marked the route."[17] This policy represented nothing more than the clumsy and excessive implementation of Secretary of War Marcy's command that "their haunts and places of rendezvous should be broken up and destroyed."[18] As evidenced by General Lane's description of the confrontation at Atlixco, the U.S. commanders remained quite willing to ruin towns as well as ranches.

The combined efforts of Lane's mounted force and Scott's garrisons established along the Veracruz–Mexico City corridor did not succeed in ending large-scale attacks by the partisans. On January 5, 1848, forces commanded by Colonel Mariano Senobio struck a convoy of 1,300 U.S. soldiers at Paso de Ovejas, Veracruz, with such force that the commanding officer, Colonel Dixon H. Miles, requested both more troops and an artillery force to fight his way through.[19] He listed his casualties in the initial attack as "one company of mounted riflemen cut up . . . and near 280 pack mules taken."[20] The Mexicans had looted the same target a day earlier. According to General David Emanuel Twiggs, a force of 100 to 400 guerrillas attacked his column near Santa Fe, Veracruz, and escaped with 250 pack mules and goods valued at between $150,000 and $200,000.[21] Given the guarantees that the convoy commanders previously issued boasting of the security provided by their troops, this particular assault proved singularly embarrassing. Subsequently, General William Orlando Butler sent an exculpatory letter to the British ambassador expressing his regret at the losses suffered by Britons who had consigned some of their goods to the convoy.[22]

In a tribute to the partisans that echoed the previously cited comments of Captain Jack Hays of the Texas Rangers, an articulate infantryman in Scott's ranks, Private Jacob J. Oswandel, observed, "During the skirmish with the infernal guerrillas, we have suffered more frightfully than at the battle of Cerro Gordo with the regular Mexican army. In fact, we would sooner face ten of the regular Mexican army than one of these outlawed guerrillas."[23]

In central México, partisans also targeted detachments far smaller than those of Twiggs or Lane. For example, Lieutenant John James Peck and his party of twenty mounted soldiers encountered a troop of guerrillas on December 11, 1847, a few miles from Puebla. The U.S. force fled without engaging.[24] On January 6, 1848, partisans killed one U.S. soldier and wounded two in the Mexico City suburb of San Angel. A U.S. counterattack left a dozen Mexicans dead.[25]

In northern México, as in the central part of the country, partisan forces vigorously attacked their foes from September 14, 1847, to February 2, 1848. On November 2, 1847, a party of 150 mounted Mexicans attacked a party of twenty U.S. Army dragoons and a few Texas Rangers some fifteen miles from Monterrey. Following the timely arrival of one hundred U.S. reinforcements, the attackers fled. After recording a description of this encounter, Taylor admitted that the Mexicans "dispersed through a country unknown to us and were able to effect their escape, or keep out of our way."[26]

On November 16, 1847, a force of 300 Mexican guerrillas assaulted a 160-man U.S. garrison at La Paz, Baja California. The sporadic siege continued for three days until the Mexicans retreated.[27] On the same day that these guerrillas ended their assault on La Paz, another group of 150 under the command of a Mexican army lieutenant, Antonio Mejares, struck nearby San José del Cabo. After deciding that U.S. reinforcements were coming ashore, the Mexicans fell back.[28] In the middle of December, Mejares again took to the offensive, albeit without success, at Mazatlán.[29]

During the final week of November 1847, Colonel Henry Burton described the Baja Californians as being in a state of "complete insurrection."

He reported a November 27 attack by a "force of about 400 men, many of them Indians," supported by an artillery piece and noted, "[M]ore than 600 people are in arms against us, and they are not to be so much despised as has been thought."[30] The U.S. Navy's senior officer in this theater of war, Commander William Branford Shubrick, conceded that unless the U.S. garrisons at the ports of Guaymas and Mazatlán received reinforcements, they would not be able to hold those positions.[31]

Attacks continued in other areas of northern México. In the states of Coahuila, Tamaulipas, and Nuevo Léon, General José Urrea's cavalry forces attacked various U.S. detachments. Their efforts culminated December 14, 1847, with a strike against a U.S. convoy. That attack at Agua Nueva, Coahuila, dispersed the 300-man force escorting the convoy and resulted in the capture of 121 wagons and 137 mules loaded with cargo. The defenders suffered many wounded and killed.[32] Here, as on other occasions, the dead included civilian wagon masters and teamsters as well as soldiers.[33] Although this Mexican commander served in the regular army rather than a patente-sanctioned guerrilla group, his tactics and mentality were those of a partisan.

In reviewing the events in northern México, a prominent group of historians led by Ramón Alcaraz concluded, "[It] appears to us that war made systematically by guerrillas would in the long run have ruined the enemy and given success to the Republic."[34] A contemporary U.S. scholar shared that respect for partisan tactics and similarly observed, "The truth is that in California and New Mexico, as in other parts of the republic, the Americans could positively claim only so much of the soil as they occupied with an army: and even that was lost as soon as deserted by a competent defensive force."[35] Months earlier, Scott had come to a similar conclusion when he confided to Taylor, "I suppose that your occupation of San Luis de Potosí, and advance upon the capital, might increase the chances of a peace or an armistice; but many intelligent persons believe that to occupy the capital and fifty other important points would not end the war, and that the enemy, without an army, would still hold out and operate against our trains, small parties, and stragglers, with rancheros on the guerrilla plan."[36]

As 1847 drew to a close, Scott's fear had become a frustrating reality. On December 12, 1847, he imposed the ultimate sanction upon the enemy: The partisans would be killed whether or not they surrendered. "No *quarters* [Scott's emphasis] will be given to known murderers or robbers whether called guerillos [*sic*] or rancheros & whether serving under Mexican commission or not. They are equally pests to unguarded Mexicans, foreigners, and small parties of Americans, and ought to be exterminated."[37] In implementing that policy, Scott duplicated on a larger scale in central México the failed policy that General John E. Wool had previously implemented in the northern state of Coahuila. In July 1847, he had decreed: "Guerrilla parties, or those who encourage them, and which I deem but highway robbers under another name, will receive no favor at the hands of the soldiers of the United States; they will be executed wherever found."[38]

Although denying quarter to one's enemies well may yield a measure of satisfaction to those who pursue such a policy, such procedures usually serve to stiffen the enemy's morale. Soldiers who believe that their surrender will be accepted hold a choice other than the dishonor of desertion or death. By contrast, combatants doomed to die may well decide to take as many of the enemy with them as possible. Such situations can prove costly to the victor as well as the vanquished. As Captain Ephraim Kirby Smith wrote in his review of the spring 1846 battle at Matamoros, Tamaulipas: "Our men, however, knew that if conquered they would receive no quarter and there was no possibility of retreat, and though surrounded by vastly superior numbers fought with determination."[39] Scott ought to have expected that Mexicans faced with a similar reality would conduct themselves as did his own forces. (Records indicate that U.S. officers in the field imposed this penalty only on a few occasions.)

Soon after Scott adopted Wool's earlier policy the latter officer invented a new tool for compelling Mexican compliance with his antipartisan efforts. From his headquarters in Monterrey, Wool proclaimed that any Mexican who "countenances or encourages, directly or indirectly, the bandits who infest the country, and who are called guerrillas must be made to feel the evils of war. Individuals will be severely punished and heavy contributions levied upon the inhabitants of all cities, towns, and villages and haciendas, who either harbor them or furnish them with supplies, or who do not give information of their haunts or places of abode."[40] Thus, Mexicans might retain their property if they served as informants. Wool soon reported to his superiors that a "number" of Mexican deputations called upon him "much alarmed, lest they be made to suffer, in consequence of robbers having visited them in times past."[41] Although the general's threat caused much consternation among civilians, no evidence indicates that they became collaborators. More importantly, the partisans continued their activities. On December 20, 1847, only three days after issuing his order threatening heavy fines, a clash between the Texas Rangers and sixty indígenas near San Miguel, Nuevo Léon, resulted in thirteen Mexican deaths. At least in the short term, the threat of collective punishment bore no fruit.

In summary, between September 14, 1847, and February 2, 1848, the U.S. Army failed to destroy the partisan forces fighting against them in the Veracruz–Mexico City corridor and in the north of México. The counter-guerrilla tactics included widespread destruction of villages, summary execution of captured partisans, collective financial punishments imposed upon municipalities, and the assignment of some 26 percent of Scott's forces to various anti-partisan duties. That campaign failed. From Veracruz to Mexico City, partisans under the command of mobile and competent leaders such as General Joaquín Rea, Juan Clímaco Rebolledo, and Padre Celedonio de Jarauta remained active in their assigned sectors of operation. Although they did not mount the same number of attacks against convoys as they did during the earlier phase of the war, they nonetheless continued to pose a strategic danger to the occupiers.

Although the U.S. Army sought futilely to counteract the partisans' success, commanders realized full well that they could not afford the consequences of provoking massive resistance on the part of Mexican civilians. Taylor's remarks about the situation in the north of México and Scott's April 1847 admonitions to his troops demonstrate that both U.S. commanders recognized that the success of their endeavors depended upon a certain minimum level of civilian passivity. Consequently, the occupiers used a two-pronged approach. Scott and his commanders sought to employ harsh measures against those who violently resisted while at the same time gaining the acquiescence, if not the cooperation, of as many other Mexicans as possible. In this regard, Scott employed a variety of political tactics to prevent the emergence of a broadly based nationalism in support of the partisan movement or any other form of continuing warfare. Secretary of War Marcy urged his generals to pursue such tactics, noting, "[I]n a country so divided into races, classes . . . there must be great room for operating on the minds and feelings of a large portion of the inhabitants, and including them to wish success to an invasion which has no desire to injure their country."[42]

In seeking to divide Mexicans, Scott first played upon religious sentiment. As previously noted, he publicly proclaimed his respect for the

Catholic faith and its practices within days of seizing Veracruz. Next, he sought to pose as a defender of the church who would protect that institution's property from hostile Mexicans. In this regard, Vice President Valentín Gómez Farías inadvertently assisted Scott. In January 1847, that erstwhile liberal had decreed the sale of as many church properties as necessary to raise 15,000,000 pesos.[43] Although Santa Anna subsequently rushed to disassociate himself from the project and sought to restore some of the confiscated property, Gómez Farías' conduct provoked a sharp response throughout México. As previously noted, two states, Oaxaca and Jalisco, flatly refused to enforce the law. In Mexico City, the armed rebellion of a national guard faction (the *Polkos*) in part resulted from Gómez's actions.[44]

Scott sought to take advantage of the lingering suspicions many devout Mexicans harbored about their government by extending the protection of his army to the church's property. On November 13, 1847, the civil and military governor of Mexico City, General John Anthony Quitman, prohibited the sale of ecclesiastical property without the consent of the U.S. Army.[45] By interposing his army between the church's property and any Mexican government that might try to seize those assets, Scott offered a blatant and significant public gesture of protection. Both the episcopacy and the numerous Mexican conservatives who had protested the actions of Gómez no doubt took some solace from the military governor's conduct. Also, those indigenous Mexicans residing upon church lands and who well might have faced eviction at the hands of new owners intent on expanding agricultural production no doubt thought a bit more kindly about their occupiers following Quitman's declaration.

Scott also sought to ensure that his troops did not offend the Catholic beliefs held by the great majority of Mexicans. In pursuit of that goal, he reminded his command, "[a]s any civilized person will never wantonly do any act to hurt the religious feelings of others, it is earnestly requested of all Protestant Americans either to keep out of the way or to pay to the Catholic religion and to its ceremonies every decent mark of respect and deference."[46] The U.S. general-in-chief and the episcopacy soon demonstrated that they could cooperate in matters of mutual benefit.

The case of some 800 soldiers and officers of the Mexican army held captive by U.S. forces in the capital illustrates this point. Scott did not want to free these prisoners because many previously released captives had violated the terms of their parole by returning to fight his forces. However, feeding and guarding 800 prisoners required considerable supplies and manpower. On November 5, 1847, Juan Manuel Irrizarri y Peralta, archbishop of Mexico City, opened an exchange with Scott in which he asked for the release of these men.[47] Five days later, the general-in-chief wrote a deferential reply offering to free the prisoners if the church would administer to those men an oath under holy sanction binding them not to take up arms again. Once released, these soldiers and officers would have no other obligation to the occupiers than to remain at peace. On December 16, 1847, the archbishop agreed to these terms. All of the prisoners received their release exactly one week later. Thus, the U.S. Army ended its burden of jailing and caring for a substantial number of prisoners while the church gained its objective of freeing those same persons. Both parties to this agreement served their own interests by serving the interest of the other.

Scott's solicitous conduct toward the Roman Catholic Church in general and toward the episcopacy in particular continued a tactic previously used by a special agent of the state department, Moses Y. Beach.[48] In Beach's report of June 14, 1847, to Secretary of State Buchanan, he claimed to have met with church officials. Beach said that he had pledged that the United States would protect the liberties and possessions of that institution and in return "found little difficulty in persuading the influential Bishops of Puebla, Guadalupe, and Michoacán through their excellent representative the Superior of the Order of St. Vincent de Paul, to refuse all aid, direct and indirect, in the prosecution of the war."[49]

As a special agent of the department of state, the enterprising Beach also sought to contact prominent Mexicans in the secular sphere who could be of use in furthering his government's objectives. Subsequently, he informed Buchanan that he found one group of federal legislators willing to consent to a new international boundary at the twenty-sixth parallel and also found considerable interest in the construction of a trans-Tehuantepec canal. However, as often proves to be the case in war, when suave words fail to persuade the citizens of an invaded nation to cooperate with the invaders, more forceful means of persuasion come to the fore.

In the case of the Catholic Church, one such incident occurred during the entrance of Scott's troops into Mexico City. When armed Mexicans began shooting at the U.S. soldiers from rooftops and windows, Scott's chief of intelligence, Colonel Hitchcock, delivered to the church the same threat he simultaneously delivered to the *ayuntamiento*. "I told one of them at the Cathedral and directed him to communicate what I said to the Senior Curate. That if the people did not cease firing, the general would [illegible] the city & give it over to plunder & further that the Churches and church property would share in the fate of the city."[50] Although the occupiers did not hesitate to use the stick rather than the carrot when such action suited their interests, Scott occasionally succeeded in cultivating good relations with Mexicans in a position to assist him. Members of the episcopacy proved to be one such group. The civilian administrators of the Mexican capital were another.

Cooperating with local officials was in the occupiers' interest. The officers of the U.S. Army did not wish to assume duties as mayors and similarly saw no benefit to be gained from assigning their soldiers to work as police officers or municipal bureaucrats, diverting them from the more important task of engaging the Mexican army and the partisans. Consequently, local officials could receive various forms of support from the invaders if they elected to cooperate. In Mexico City, the first such gesture proved to be quite substantial. Scarcely a week after the fall of the city, Quitman issued a proclamation: "The municipal authorities of the City and district will retain all their usual sources of revenue. . . . En [sic] addition thereto, the internal customs on duties which have heretofore been collected at the Custom House, City Gate, and Elsewhere are for the present surrendered to the Ayuntamiento."[51] Thus, the capital's government not only retained its traditional sources of income, but also received monies formerly collected by the national government. Fortified with that revenue, the city officials could continue their work. Perhaps no group of municipal workers were more important than the police. If they functioned effectively, then the U.S. forces would be relieved of a duty for which they were not linguistically or otherwise prepared. For any police force to succeed in its mission, the officers and their authority must be respected. Quitman told his commanders: "Soldiers and followers of the army who shall be found ill treating said police in the lawful discharge of their duties, will be regarded as serious offenders and severely punished."[52]

Participants from both sides of the warring armies commented upon the extent to which many of the capital's higher social elements did not exhibit the same hostility to the invaders as did the partisans in the countryside. When Santa Anna entered the city just after the horrific battles in which thousands of common Mexicans perished, he bitterly observed the contrast between their ultimate sacrifice and the conduct of the city's elite: "I recognized that here passed the *hombres de bien*, the cowards and colluders with the invader, not able to tolerate any longer the evils of war, and that sooner or later, their intrigue and their skilled hands would sacrifice me without public use to satisfy political passions."[53] A Mexican historian who recorded the entrance of the victorious army into Mexico City angrily wrote that many of the city's most affluent citizens hung the flags of foreign governments from their residences as the U.S. Army marched forward: "In these moments, the rich class manifested their cowardice. México appeared as a work of Mount Parnassus, with all of the balconies covered with flags in diverse colors and combinations. . . . What ought we to hope for the country, with a debased generation, who in the hour of danger were ashamed to be of Mexican birth?"[54]

The apparent apathy and fear with which some of the capital's politically active citizens regarded the invaders easily developed into more supportive sentiments when the two sides could be of use to each other. Such a situation occurred during Mexico City's municipal elections of late 1847. To conform to precedent and to legitimize their continued presence in office, the Moderado faction of the liberals, which controlled the ayuntamiento initially decided to proceed with the elections. However, the national government had declared that no balloting ought to take place in territory occupied by the enemy. Since both the federal authorities in the temporary national capital of Querétaro and the municipal authorities in Mexico City belonged to the faction of the liberals, the latter deferred to the former and cancelled the election. This presented the minority faction within the liberal ranks, the Puros, with a splendid opportunity. They realized that while a majority of the party's members did not share their fierce hostility to the church and to the army, the minority faction nonetheless

could win control of the city government if the Moderados did not participate in the balloting. Consequently, they met on December 5, 1847, and
chose electors. They claimed authority to do so under the provision of laws
requiring that elections be held on that date. Obviously, the fact that
Moderados did not participate in this process meant that the newly chosen
electors reflected a far more radical consensus than did the existing ayuntamiento. Rather than accept this *fait accompli*, the city government sched-
uled an alternate ballot to choose electors on December 19, 1847, with the
actual election of council members to take place one week later. Thus,
Mexico City might have begun 1848 with two duly constituted governments.

At that point, the U.S. military governor intervened and announced
that he would designate the proper victors. In doing so, Brigadier General
Persifor Frazer Smith, the second U.S. military governor of Mexico City,
declared that December 5, 1847, the election date stipulated by law was
the valid one. Of the twenty-two seats in the city council, he assigned only
one to a member of the previous government.[55] Clearly, the Puros owed
their newly dominant position to the occupiers. Smith's conduct provided
a fine example of Marcy's admonition to take advantage of internal dissen-
sion to weaken Mexican hostility to the United States. The Puros wished
to use the occupiers just as the occupiers had used them. At a lavish ban-
quet in honor of Scott, members of the newly installed government
declared their preferences: "The Mexicans offered . . . grave toasts all of
which were decidedly friendly to the U.S. Army & in two or three cases the
Mexicans in so many words hoped we would not leave the country until
we should first destroy the influence of the clergy and the military."[56] The
Puros of that day shared at least one sentiment with their foes in the city's
episcopacy. Both were quite willing to cooperate with the invader to achieve
their objectives.

Other municipalities also exercised considerable autonomy in the performance of their duties as long as they offered the invaders such cooperation as they wished. For example, in Xalapa the municipal cabildo raised its revenues, debated its priorities, allocated its funds, and tended to the usual myriad of local concerns with only the slightest interference from the occupiers.[57] The minutes of the municipal cabildo taken during the occupation indicate that on only one occasion did the U.S. military governor countermand the cabildo, and that matter involved a proposed expansion of the municipal police force. Although the occupiers also requested a substantial contribution from the cabildo, records do not indicate whether they ever received the money. Similarly, the city's three successive military governors proved amenable to some requests of the local council. For example, when the councilors asked that the quartermaster of the garrison find a secure and heavily walled location for his munitions other than the parish church, the U.S. commander complied.[58]

Xalapa's leading citizens appreciated the light hand of their temporary governors and reciprocated. When the Mexican government sent the town councilors a request to strengthen the partisan forces, these leading citizens demurred.[59] Lest the partisans themselves be in any doubt, their commander was invited to a meeting at which the council did little more than ask him to conclude an agreement restraining the conduct of his men.

While the Xalapan leaders no doubt disliked the occupation of their national territory, they undeniably also received some benefits from it. The course of war severely limited the ability of México's government to threaten its own citizens. But the ongoing destruction of the regime's troops gradually exposed a far more severe chasm in the national polity. Since the earliest days of México's independence, the army constituted the most devastating response to agrarian rebellion against the socio-economic and political elite that governed México. When the negotiating skills of Álvarez failed, and after the efforts of the local police and a state's own soldiers proved inadequate, hacendados and hombres de bien utilized the army. By late 1847, much of that army no longer existed. In this environment, pueblos across México intensified their rebellions. These guerrillas identified the owners of large estates and the national government as their primary enemies and relegated U.S. troops to the category of secondary menace. Campesino rebellions continued in numerous locations, without national coordination.

In November 1847, General Francisco de Garay confirmed that "insurrectional movement of indigenous people in the district of Veracruz" had erupted and that rebels intended to march on Ozuluama.[60] In explaining the objectives of the indigenous rebels, he stated that they sought the restoration of "rights they believe they have to lands possessed by some of the hacienda proprietors."[61] The bases of these rebels were the pueblos of Amatlán, Tancoco, and San Antonio, all of which were in proximity to Tampico. On January 3, 1848, they summarized their objectives in a manifesto, demanding the "derecognition of all authorities of the government, leaving the people in liberty to choose their employment, preferring, to the extent in which it is possible, the most illustrious indígena class."[62] Thus, the rebels defined themselves as both an ethnicity (indigenous Mexicans) and as a class (laborers).

Also, their demands incorporated the Mesoamerican concept of communal as opposed to individual land ownership first advanced by the Spaniards. They declared, "The collection of land rents is absolutely prohibited, and in consequence, from now and henceforth, the haciendas are declared common, to be enjoyed in common without stipend."[63] In seeking to rid themselves of other practices associated with the national state, they demanded the repeal of all non-war-related taxes and the abolition of fees paid directly to the church for services rendered by priests.[64]

Perhaps the most critical part of this manifesto is the offer of military assistance given by the villagers. They pledged to render loyal service to México if the regime acceded to the above-cited demands. Thus, their loyalty to the state rested upon the restoration of their pre-conquest rights. Here, the two Méxicos confronted each other over a fundamental dispute about the social order that remained unresolved three centuries after the Spanish invasion. Understandably, the national government placed no priority on dismantling the social structure that supported its existence.

In Veracruz and in other states, the remaining Mexican army did not possess the force necessary to reestablish its rule over such pueblos. A mere two days after Garay completed his report, a federal cabinet minister explained to the commissioner of the state of Tamaulipas that he did not have the troops necessary to remedy the ruination of several unspecified pueblos. Instead, he suggested the use of the national guard.[65] In Zacatecas, a member of the state's legislative deputation vaguely acknowledged the situation as one in which "a nearby incursion of barbarous Indians has introduced a considerable number of them into some of the pueblos of Durango."[66] Zacatecas and Durango and Veracruz lay some distance from the national capital.

However, the state of México bordered the country's administrative center. Consequently rebellions there posed a more direct threat to the regime. In the Mexiquense (state of México) villages of Temascaltepec, Sultepec, and Zacualpan, revolts targeting officials and property were underway by the final week of January 1848.[67] During that same week, the adjacent state of Puebla reported that an outbreak of activity by "subversives" necessitated the dispatch of fifty national guard troops to the pueblo of Huachinango.[68] The neighboring communities of Chicontepec and Tantoyuca also required a similar response. The residents of the two latter villages issued a manifesto. The Plan de Tantoyuca y Chicontepec contained several interesting points. The authors began by calling on all Mexicans to fight the invaders in an "equal and just manner."[69] Then they set forth their domestic agenda: "Because in the war which we have, the United States has as its object the domination and despoliation of our territory, which we cannot recover without the cooperation of all Mexicans, it is declared that all of the national territory will be common to all citizens of the republic."[70] Here, as in Amatlán, the campesinos wove together the defense of the ancient concept of communal land ownership with the more modern concept of the nation-state.

In the Yucatán, the indígena and campesino rebels took advantage of a split in the ranks of rival elites to begin a sustained uprising in July 1847.[71] The rebels found widespread support, particularly because the Indians lived under conditions in many respects indistinguishable from slavery. The accelerating breadth and ferocity of the rebellion drew increasing attention from the national government during succeeding months. Although the Mexican government refered to this conflict as the Caste War because of the Maya's low social status, this conflict would be defined by those same officials a racial conflict.

Unlike the revolt of Amatlán, the Yucatecans sought more than the restoration of pre-conquest patterns of land ownership: They sought nothing less than the expulsion of the descendants of the colonists who lived among them. Also, the Maya rebels of Yucatán coordinated their activities on a peninsula-wide basis, and their struggle consequently encompassed all of that territory. Even though some of that region's rulers thought of their land as being distinct from the rest of México, those Mexicans governing the nation knew from past experience that indígena rebellions did not respect political demarcations drawn in the national capital. One 1848 report confirmed that a delegation of Maya entered the state of Oaxaca seeking allies among other tribes.[72]

A second and related aspect of México's domestic revolts fell under the rubric of banditry and social chaos. As used here, banditry refers to non-political violence directed against individuals, governments, or societal targets. In the absence of a minimally staffed and funded police force, national guard, or army, such activities flourish luxuriantly. As early as September 1847, the violence in and around the city of Puebla accelerated to a level that General Joaquín Rea and the U.S. civil and military governor of the city, Lieutenant Colonel Thomas Childs, met under a flag of truce to discuss a coordinated response.[73] The Mexican commander stated, "I am anxious that all robbers and disorderly persons should be kept out of the city and that quiet and order should be enjoyed by the citizens." His counterpart stated that he shared that goal.[74] Rea then suggested that his men be allowed to guard the gates of the city: "Thousands of men come into the city, professing to belong to my commands with whom I have nothing to do. If I can be permitted to guard the gates, I will pledge my honor that my troops will not interfere with the Americans. . . . If it is objectionable to have my troops at the gates, I would be willing to occupy the roads leading to the city, at a distance of two to three leagues."[75] Although Childs declined to co-sign a written proposal to this effect, the two commanders nonetheless came to an informal understanding. The Mexican general indeed would keep the road to the U.S. Army camp clear and allow supplies to enter the city.

While the transcript of these negotiations confirms the extent to which banditry concerned officials of both nations, that conversation between Childs and Rea also provides evidence of an additional crisis. Rea's characterization of thousands of men entering the city indicates a large transient population. The previously referenced U.S. policy of scorching the earth in an effort to eliminate partisan depots inevitably would have generated a considerable number of homeless—and no doubt embittered—Mexicans. The emphasis upon maintaining order became a theme of many communities. The Mexiquenses who comprised the Toluca city council declared on January 4, 1848, that public tranquility remained "the talisman that absorbed the attention of this municipal body."[76] Leading Tolucans feared assault and robbery. In Xalapa, the cabildo expressed on August 5, 1847, the "indispensable" need to assure the safety of the city.[77]

On some occasions, the perpetrators of various crimes against innocent Mexican citizens were not deserters or criminals, but undisciplined partisans. In November 1847, the *Comandancia* (command headquarters) of the Veracruz state government complained of partisans' perpetrating "frequent disorders" and committing crimes against both "peaceful inhabitants" and property in the course of fighting the U.S. Army.[78] One week later, Mariano Senobio, commander of the Linea de Guerrillas de Caliente, noted that he was taking measures to combat thieves who were "committing disorders" in the name of guerrillas.[79] During that same month, the Xalapa cabildo requested the revocation of the patente of José Nuñez Villavicencio for unspecified excesses.[80] In the northern state of Nuevo Léon, the state government requested that identical action be taken against another guerrilla and patente-holder, Norvento Galán, on the grounds that he perpetrated an "infamous system of depredation" utilizing "lost men, without occupation, vagabonds and criminals" to commit robbery."[81] Depredations committed by partisans under military command became so frequent that by October 1847, the president of the republic directly ordered the general commanding this area to "severely punish" all crimes committed by guerrillas in the government's service.[82]

In Guanajuato, Governor Lorenzo Arellano took action far more vigorous than merely requesting federal assistance. In December 1847, he declared that because of the "consequences of the actual circumstances of agitation in which the Republic finds itself and because of the multitude of army deserters who roam in all parts, today found in the population, the camps and ways, infested with thieves, [and] evil-doers," he would form an armed unit separate and distinct from the national guard. In his decree, the governor ordered owners of rural estates (*fincas rusticas*) to provide one man for each 50,000 pesos of assets owned for this force.[83] Arellano's decision to limit enlistments to those deemed trustworthy by men of property speaks of an enduring criollo mentality. This type of recruitment implicitly assumed that a typical campesino or ranchero was not worthy of trust. Also, Arellano's decision to raise an armed body of men responsible to "the Governor and the political chiefs" without reference to the authority of the state legislature exemplifies the *caudillismo* typical of much of early Mexican history.[84] Finally, by listing agitation as well as theft among the reasons that compelled him to organize this armed force, he conceded that emerging dissent was a significant concern. For him, political agitation ranked at the same level as robbery.[85]

Perhaps the grimmest portent of the nation's future could be read in the description of the state of affairs in Tlaxcala. On December 21, 1847, the minister of hacienda stated, "In a word, there is in the territory perfect anarchy."[86] The problems he cited included guerrillas and other military forces that existed solely to extort money from the pueblos, "scandalous

disobedience" to the government including a loss of revenue, and depredations committed by counter-guerrillas.[87] In a similar vein, Álvarez noted
during late January that one of his units found itself involved in combat
against both rebellious Mexicans and U.S. troops.[88] So in the first months
of 1848, Mexican partisans fought the foreign foe; Mexican peasants
fought their nation's rulers; and México's government proved incapable of
controlling either the foreign or domestic foe. The prospect of the situation
degenerating into a war of all against all seemed quite genuine. But before
that happened, the two national governments signed a peace treaty.

CHAPTER FIVE

UNITED
AGAINST THE MAJORITY

Both politically and commercially, we have the deepest interest
in her [México's] regeneration and prosperity. Indeed,
it is impossible that, with any just regard to our own safety,
we can ever become indifferent to her fate.

JAMES K. POLK

For many, the signing of the Treaty of Guadalupe Hidalgo on February 2, 1848, marked the end of the war. In this construct, the fighting ceased and the U.S. Army remained in México while the two nations subsequently agreed to minor changes in this pact. Following the joint ratification of the revised treaty, the invaders departed, and the conflict receded into the past. That notion, however, is incomplete and inaccurate.

Although the treaty and the subsequent armistice of March 6, 1848, ended the violence between the two national armies, other armed conflicts occurring throughout México did not cease. During the remainder of that year, campesino and indígena alienation continued to explode into geographically diffuse rebellions against the Mexican government. The United States responded to these uprisings by aiding the elite that stood at the apex of México's socio-economic and political structure. The United

States did so because the continued existence of that regime remained a necessity for both the legitimization of U.S. territorial conquest and for the establishment of a cooperative post-war Mexican government.

The only violence ended by the treaty and the consequent armistice was the conflict between those forces under the commands of the two national governments. The major guerrilla formations along the Veracruz–Mexico City line served under officers authorized to command by the provisions of Substitute President Pedro Maria Anaya's proclamation of April 28, 1847.[1] Only those deemed loyal to the state and the social order had received permission to lead these units. With just two exceptions, their commanders complied with the terms of the armistice.

From February 2, 1848, until the final U.S. withdrawal on September 6, 1848, substantial partisan forces attacked only two supply trains. On February 18, 200 Mexican lancers blocked a force of ninety U.S. Army cavalry escorting several wagons from Veracruz to Orizaba. After estimating the total Mexican force in the immediate vicinity to be between 400 and 500 men, Lieutenant Walter L. Biscoe rapidly returned to Veracruz. He set his own losses at five men slain while claiming twenty-five partisan deaths.[2] In the far north during that same month, a guerrilla force estimated at 500 New Mexicans, Apaches, and Comanches attacked a U.S. column of at least 200 troops in the vicinity of El Paso.[3] The Mexicans killed twenty soldiers, took most of the mules and horses, and killed the oxen. The U.S. troops abandoned their wagons.

Although both of these attacks took place after the February 2, 1848, signing of the peace treaty, they nonetheless occurred before the subsequent armistice agreement was signed on March 6, 1848. After that date, Mexican guerrillas no longer challenged any large U.S. convoy. For example, on April 16, 1848, a train of some 400 wagons, 3,500 pack mules, and 450 sick and wounded soldiers reached Veracruz from Mexico City having "experienced no opposition from guerilleros or others."[4] By contrast, the convoys traveling the same route in 1847 had suffered substantial and repeated attacks. Two days after the arrival of this convoy, a return train of 3,000 pack mules, 200 wagons, and an artillery battery also traveled that same route without being attacked.[5]

Clearly, most of the light corps commanders of the Mexican army who operated along the Veracruz–Mexico City corridor obeyed their orders to cease hostilities. Some did so with great regret. One partisan commander and army general, Joaquín Rea, found himself so embittered by this turn of events that he requested his passport to leave "our moribund patria," whose defense "we had abandoned."[6] However, two of the light corps commanders did not comply with the armistice and continued to fight independently of the campesino-based agrarian rebels. Most prominently, Padre Celedonio de Jarauta and Manuel Montano denounced the peace treaty and vowed to remain at war. Even after suffering severe losses at the hands of a U.S. force on February 28, 1848, Jarauta led 300 cavalry and fifty infantry into Zacualtipán, México, and proclaimed his intention to continue the war. He then stole assets worth half a million pesos to support his military operations.[7] Yet both Jarauta and Montano refused to align themselves with the indígena rebels. Instead, they forged an alliance with General Mariano Paredes y Arrillaga, an authoritarian and centralist conservative sympathetic to the cause of monarchy who also violently opposed the peace treaty.

With all of the light corps commanders except Jarauta and Montano at rest, the U.S. Army consequently required far fewer resources to maintain communications along the Veracruz–Mexico City route than had once been the case. On February 22, 1848, the American command inaugurated a monthly mail run from the national capital to the main seaport with an escort of twenty-five men throughout the journey.[8] The smaller groups of autonomous guerrillas that emerged along this corridor after March 1848 lacked the capacity to attack these mail trains, let alone the far larger convoys. As a result, they focused their assaults upon U.S. detachments of a few dozen men or less. Even this reduced level of violence represented an obstacle to the reestablishment of the social order sought by both governments. Scott's replacement, General William Orlando Butler ordered "the line from the City of Mexico to Vera Cruz [sic] to be held and vigorous measures to be taken to clear the guerrilla parties."[9]

In early and mid-1848, the momentum of events was fueled by the large number of Mexicans in rebellion against the state and the elite who comprised its base of power. As early as February of that year, many of the poor people of color who constituted the great mass of the nation had moved past sentiments of alienation into outright rebellion. These rebels stood apart from the commanders of the formidable partisan units who once threatened the U.S. Army supply line running from the gulf to the capital. Officials at the highest levels of Mexican society rightly feared a civil war along lines of race and class. In some parts of the nation, such conflicts indeed erupted. By the end of 1848, the depth and ferocity of these rebellions proved so intense that 21,278 federal troops fought guerrillas in the Huasteca, the Sierra Gorda, Puebla, México state, and the Yucatán.[10] By comparison, the total number of troops deployed against the U.S. Army during the battles for the Valley of México never exceeded 20,000 soldiers.[11]

Of the many revolts taking place, the coordinated uprising that engulfed the Yucatán caused the greatest concern. There, rebels mobilized a predominantly Mayan force that totaled 30,000 combatants.[12] The governor, Miguel Barbachano, declared his own administration "in absolute impotence to resist" a rebellion taking on the "character of a war of exter-mination against the white race."[13] The ferocity and size of the Yucatecan rebellion flowed from the unique cultural and political circumstances of this region.

Like the central valley of México, the Yucatán served as the territorial base for one of the nation's two great pre-Columbian civilizations. However, the Mayan political structure rested not upon one great political center such as Tenochtitlán, but upon dozens of Yucatecan cities that func-tioned as independent political and military centers. Consequently, the Spanish could neither conquer the peninsula simply by taking the largest city nor smash Yucatecan resistance by decimating a particular polity. Lengthy and costly campaigns in both jungles and cities were necessary before the colonial government could claim any sort of sovereignty.

Both prior to and after independence, Yucatecan hacendados main-tained a system of debt peonage in an effort to bind their indigenous work-force to rapidly expanding sugar and *henequen* industries.[14] Even Maya not newly bound to the hacienda resented the seizure of lands they believed to be the sacred realm of their deities. Here, as in the territories that would be engulfed by the Álvarez Rebellion, indigenous anger gradually increased. Then in 1841, a uniquely Yucatecan series of events began.

At that time, liberal and federalist members of the region's elite pro-claimed a new constitution. Two years later, centralist forces under Santa Anna threatened to overrun the peninsula. In response, the state's govern-ment armed thousands of indígenas, promising them land and release from taxes in return for service against the national government. The Maya responded, slaying many of the invading soldiers. Following Santa Anna's failure to take the main port of Campeche, the criollo rebels obtained the autonomy they sought from Mexico City and the assurance that their state militia would not be sent to fight foreign wars. In return, they acknowledged the Mexican state's sovereignty over Yucatán. The triumphant criollos promptly reneged on their commitment to the armed Mayans whose efforts had made possible their triumph.[15] A palpable sense of rage spread through the indigenous ranks.

In 1847, a criollo junta seized control of Mérida, raising the specter of violent conflict between the rival elites of that city and of Campeche. With their criollo masters divided and México itself under invasion, the Maya erupted in a peninsula-wide rebellion. With fierce grievances and a level of organization far greater than those of the partisans of other rebellious indígenas, the Yucatecan combat veterans spearheaded a campaign that succeeded in driving the criollos from much of the peninsula.

Faced with such dire prospects, the state government sought help from all quarters. On March 7, 1848, Justo Sierra O'Reilly, the Yucatecan commissioner to the United States, submitted a request for military intervention to the highest level of the U.S. government.[16] However, scarcely more than two weeks later, the governor of Yucatán considered the situation so catastrophic that he offered the United States "dominion and sovereignty of the Peninsula."[17] He described the situation: "The white race, the civilized class of this State, is now attacked in an atrocious and barbarous manner by the aboriginal caste, which rising simultaneously, in insurrection, by an instinct of ferocity, is making a savage and exterminating war upon us." [18] At a meeting April 15, 1848, Polk and Buchanan discussed these two solicitations. Understandably, they could not find any compelling reason to involve their nation's soldiers in this conflict. However, the United States did provide some materiel. During April, Commodore Matthew C. Perry left Veracruz with a shipment of arms and munitions for "the use of the whites in protecting themselves from the Indians."[19]

As an additional inducement to foreigners, the state's highest officials asked Great Britain, France, and the United States for help and in return offered to "surrender their country and sovereignty over it to any government which would protect & save them from extermination."[20] Like Polk, the British and French saw no reason to involve their armies in this matter. The shipload of supplies that the United States sent did not reverse the tide of the rebellion. In June 1848, 2,000 indígenas at the pueblo of Tlampolon repelled an attacking force of 350 state troops, killing 150 of those soldiers in the process.[21]

In that same month, the Mexican government responded to the deteriorating situation in the Yucatán and in other parts of the nation by repeating Sierra's efforts to obtain the services of U.S. soldiers for a counterguerrilla campaign. In pursuit of that goal, México's ministry of foreign relations sent to Washington, D.C., an experienced envoy, Francisco Arrangoiz. The U.S. secretary of state described the ensuing events: "On the same day, he [Arrangoiz] called at the Department, presented his credentials, and informed me of his mission. He said that it was the desire of the Mexican government that the United States should furnish to México three or four thousand troops, to be employed, in the first place, against the Indians of Yucatán, and if need be, against Indians in other portions of México. In case of necessity, they would, also, be employed to sustain the present government against the revolutionists."[22] Under the terms of this proposal, U.S. soldiers would receive their usual pay and rations with expenses being paid from the funds that México was to receive on May 30, 1849. Polk quickly rejected the proposal, writing that, as president, he did not possess the authority to deploy the army outside of his own nation's territory without the permission of the Senate.[23] He did not commit to paper several equally obvious points: His army's recent efforts fighting partisan warfare had not been wholly successful, and he wished to bring the war with México to a rapid conclusion.

Arrangoiz's proposal cited the potential use of U.S. troops not only against the Maya in the Yucatán, but in other areas of the nation as well. Minister Luis de la Rosa deemed the Huasteca a region in which the use of foreign troops would be of benefit and expressed his fear that the situation in Huastecan communities could become as serious as that in the vicinity of the Mexiquense pueblo of Ozuluama, in which "dreadful bloody assassination engulfed entire populations."[24] He also feared that the rebellions in that pueblo and in Techanhuitla, rural Veracruz, and Tuxpan could spread to the adjacent cities of Mexico City, Veracruz, San Luis Potosí, and Puebla.[25] He believed that "the war of death and of extermination that the subversives have declared on the white class [*clase blanca*] and the well-to-do, the ramification that the revolution has in all the pueblos, for the majority of their inhabitants are comprised of rugged indígenas who grow stronger as they acquire [more], and the small force that has few arms, [illegible] call for my immediate attention."[26]

Also, Rosa flatly warned that these rebellions in central México held the potential to reach the level of the revolts taking place in the Sierra Gorda region of Yucatán.[27] He recommended the suppression of the Huastecan rebels, and the regime subsequently dispatched some of its scarce infantry to Huehuetla. Here as in other locations, some of the national guard units that ostensibly existed to support the established social order had proved to be of questionable loyalty and consequently of little use to the central government.[28] In the case of Huehuetla, the officer reporting to the minister of war and marine attributed the national guard's inaction to the sympathy of some of its members with the rebels.

Minister Rosa received reports of similar outbursts of violence in other areas of central México. In the Sierra Gorda, rebels forces totaled 2,000.[29] In the adjoining state of Querétaro, the comandancia general reported the transformation of an indigenous movement from a group "ostensibly" begun to defend Mexicans into a force to act "against the white race."[30]

In some instances, the inability of the army to attack the rebels remained much the same as before the signing of the armistice. From the Veracruz prefecture of Tuxpan and Chicontepec, Captain Anastasio Llorente regretfully told his superior that virtually no troops stood ready to restore order.[31] In 1847, Llorente had received authorization to lead a light corps unit against Scott's forces along the Veracruz–Mexico City corridor. Yet in 1848, he fought fellow Mexicans. According to Llorente, the situation in the adjacent state of Puebla was little better. He described the need to return entire villages "to order and reestablish authority."[32] His major concerns included the presence of a rebel force of 800 men at Huatla during May 1848.[33]

The U.S. Army fought against a few of these rebel groups. The sixteenth article of the armistice agreement of May 6, 1848, between the two nations obligated the occupiers to a limited form of involvement against these campesinos. "If any body of armed men be assembled in any part of the Mexican Republic with a view of committing hostilities not authorized by either government, it shall be the duty of either or both of the contracting parties to oppose and disperse such body; without considering those who compose it."[34] At the time that the two nations signed this armistice, the U.S. Army occupied major cities throughout México including the national capital and Acapulco, Camargo, Monterrey, Puebla, Saltillo, Tampico, and Veracruz. In the event that any indigenous rebellion grew to the point at which rebels attacked any of those cites, the soldiers stationed there would have no alternative than to defend those cites. Thus, México's major centers of population acquired two sets of defenders. The U.S. Army did not add to this obligation by systematically seeking encounters with the rebellious indígenas. Clashes that did occur between the two sides seem to have taken place principally as a result of decisions made by individual U.S. officers in proximity to a particular rebellious pueblo or region.

Major Folliot T. Lally described one such encounter, noting that during the first week of April 1848 he received reports of attacks on citizens of the pueblo of Ozuluama. In response, Lally dispatched a captain with sixty cavalry to "restore order and peace . . . for the sake of humanity."[35] During the following week, he received an additional request for armed intervention from "some highly respectable citizens of Huasteca (100 miles south of this)," who wanted him to "send a force of two or three hundred men to repel the savages thereabout, who are making war upon the peaceful, unoffending people of that part of the country, by killing and driving off all whom they meet, besides burning and destroying property."[36] Though Lally wished to comply with this request, he hesitated to do so simply because Huasteca lay twice as far from his Tampico base as did Ozuluama. Consequently, he requested authorization to send a force of one hundred infantry and fifty cavalry to the petitioners' aid. There is no record of his having received approval for the proposed expedition.

Lally identified the primary cause of the warfare between Mexicans: "The hostile Indians have set up a claim to the land in that section of the country based upon the right of being the original owners prior to the invasion of Cortés, but do not design to war with the United States. They are, however, lawless and barbarous, and have for several months been savage in their progress through this part of the country where the towns of Huejutla, Huasteca, and Osiliwama [sic] lay."[37] While Lally's description of the rebels' objective mirrors that of many other indígena uprisings in México, his summary of the situation differs from that of Rosa and Barbachano in one key regard. Lally describes the conflict's primary catalyst as a desire for land. By contrast, the criollos' descriptions focus first upon the issue of race, then of land.

Several U.S. commanders similarly involved themselves in ongoing civil war in the Cuernavaca district. Here too, indígenas rose in rebellion. Once again, U.S. soldiers engaged their new enemy on behalf of the Mexican state. Colonel Newman S. Clarke described the struggle: "On the 11th instant rumors reached here of an assembling of Indígenas for mischievous purposes at St. Vicente and Sochatepec. They were succeeded by other rumors of an intention on their part not only to prevent supplies from entering the city, but to attack the various Haciendas in the vicinity of those places."[38] In response, Clarke "detached Major Miller 1st infantry with a large portion of his Regiment to the last named village and Captain Gardiner of the Regiment to the first-named village with orders to attack and capture or destroy any Guerilleros [sic] or *ladrones* [thieves] they might encounter."[39] Somewhat cryptically, the colonel stated that after a night march, his soldiers "dispersed the bodies of men lawlessly assembled and returned, the former on the evening of Friday last and the latter on Saturday."[40] Clarke's decision to forgo any mention of casualties inflicted or captives taken by a force ordered to "attack and capture or destroy any guerilleros [sic] or ladrones they might encounter" remains puzzling. However, this U.S. colonel by no means deemed the situation in these two villages to be isolated incidents. Indeed, he wrote of widespread rebellions: "But however, an insurrectionary spirit is said to pervade some twenty-seven or less Indigenous villages fomented by one Arillano [sic], a noted Brigand or Guerrilla. The avowed object is the encroachment upon the haciendas mostly owned by whites and Spaniards & said Arillano has artfully it is supposed [to have] propagated the notion that the North Americans are favorable to his pretexts and that under such circumstances the ignorant and the [illegible] Indians may attempt to recover their land."[41] Captain Samuel P. Heintzelman provided a brief summary of his own involvement in deployments against the rebels: "On the other line, I have pursued the Indians and taken from them their booty but I believe that this is the first time we have joined our implacable enemies [the Mexican army] to put down them."[42]

Also, U.S. troops attacked rebels at the Hacienda Oguada in the Ozuluama district. They happened to be passing by the estate (*que pasada casualmente*) as a force of "subversives" looted the property.[43] The district police commander claimed that he personally pursued the rebels, who then dispersed in three directions. The Mexican commander estimated the size of the rebel force in the area to be 150 men under the leadership of one Pedro Hernández, based in Chontla. The armies of both nations were unable to protect all of the great estates in the Cuernavaca area. In early March, 300 indígenas attacked the Chiconcaque hacienda, forcing the administrator and his servants to take shelter in a tower.[44]

Thus U.S. forces directly involved themselves in combat against rebellious indígenas and peasants only when such opportunities presented themselves and the commanding officers sought to involve their forces. Conversely the rebellious peasants, whom both governments feared, did not primarily attack the U.S. Army. As Lally correctly stated, they instead focused their hostility upon the Mexican government and its principal rural patrons, the hacendados. Both the guerrillas and the occupiers preferred a loose rather than strict interpretation of article sixteen of the armistice agreement.

In their dispatches, some U.S. officers referred to the rebels as thieves. This in turn raises the question of whether or not the indígenas were engaging in genuine rebellion or social banditry of the sort described by British historian Eric Hobsbawm. He defined the latter sort of conduct as "endemic peasant protest against oppression and poverty, a cry for vengeance on the rich and the oppressors, a vague dream of some curb upon them, a righting of individual wrongs."[45] The rebels of 1848 were not social bandits. Unlike the individuals characterized by Hobsbawm, these Mexicans had clear goals in mind. They repeatedly proclaimed their objectives in statements such as the Plan de Tantoyuca y Chicontepec and the Manifesto of Amatlan: the restoration of communal land holdings and the consequent end of the hacienda system. Possessing specific political and economic objectives, they should not be classified with Hobsbawm's prepolitical bandits engaging in unfocused violence or as thieves utilizing the chaos created by war to embark on an aimless crime spree.

Few guerrillas of any category sought combat with the U.S. Army during the spring and summer of 1848. Those partisans who attacked U.S. troops confined their efforts to small and isolated parties of soldiers. In May 1848, partisans trapped twenty-five American soldiers at Agua Fría, Chihuahua. Although one hundred U.S. cavalrymen subsequently galloped to the rescue of the encircled party, the partisans killed seven men and wounded ten. Mexican fatalities totaled twenty-nine.[46] The remaining reports of armed clashes between the U.S. Army and Mexicans during this period all involved fewer than a dozen U.S. soldiers. For example, on March 28, 1848, Captain Kenton Harper reported from Parras, Coahuila, the deaths of two U.S. soldiers. He further noted that he had ordered the execution of a Mexican who confessed to participating in the killing of these men.[47] Following the murder of several U.S. citizens in Mexico

City, the editors of *The American Star* urged their countrymen to carry arms when entering those suburbs.[48]

To their credit, and in the interest of minimizing the hostility of the populace, some senior officers tried to restrain the excesses of their own troops during this period. At Orizaba, the commanding officer of the U.S. garrison responded to a Mexican citizen's charge that soldiers had robbed him by posting an order stating that any soldier found committing robbery would be disciplined for disobedience of orders and forced to pay for the stolen property.[49] From Monterrey, General Wool declared he considered the "deserters . . . and dishonorably discharged soldiers" who committed "every species of atrocity on the defenseless inhabitants" to be so vile that he ordered his subordinates to "make all possible exertions to apprehend the villains and bring them to punishment."[50]

However, from the signing of the armistice on March 6, 1848, until the departure of the last U.S. troops in September of that year, what most altered the relationships among occupiers, the occupied, and the various guerrillas was the United States' decision to supply armaments to the Mexican government. On June 7, 1848, the U.S. sold the Mexican government 5,125 rifles and cartridge belts, 762,400 rifle cartridges, 208 carbines with 30,000 carbine cartridges, and 124 fulminating rifles with 87,500 cartridges.[51] The U.S. Army sold some of this equipment at deeply discounted prices. For example, they charged the Mexicans ten pesos per rifle even though the market price quoted by Santiago Humphrey in his guerrilla budget (Table 2.2) was twice that figure.

In July 1848, the United States once again disposed of a substantial amount of infantry equipment on generous terms. General Frazer Smith, the last U.S. military governor of Mexico City, ordered his subordinates "to deliver to the Mexican Government, Señor Don Francisco Arrangoiz, all muskets remaining on hand, at the ordnance depot; and two hundred thousand flint musket cartridges: together with muskets and accoutrements turned in by the 12th & 14th Regiments Infantry and 1st Regt. of Artillery."[52] Interestingly, Arrangoiz, the Mexican agent designated to facilitate this matter, had been sent by México to Washington one month earlier to negotiate the services of 4,000 U.S. soldiers against the Yucatecan rebels. Although he had returned from that mission without the concession he sought, Arrangoiz nonetheless gained access to U.S. arms. In these transactions, the United States' priority consisted of arming the Mexican state rather than merely disposing of U.S. property. Smith made that point quite clear to his subordinate: "Previous to delivery you will agree with the agent on the prices to be paid to the United States for Said Military Stores, by the Mexican Government; and furnish him, finally, with Invoices of the articles he received, with the prices offered, and take from the corresponding receipts."[53] In other words, the delivery would take place with the price being merely a procedural matter.

U.S. commanders in both the northern and central parts of the country transferred additional military assets to the Mexican army under article four of the Treaty of Guadalupe Hidalgo. This provision required the U.S. Army to return "all castles, forts, territories, places and possessions . . . within the limits of the Mexican Republic . . . together with all the artillery, arms, apparatus of war, munitions, and other public property, which were in said castles and forts."[54] At Monterrey, this equipment consisted of twenty-seven brass cannons firing twelve-pound shot and three howitzers.[55] Robert E. Lee gave one indication of the amount of weaponry involved in these transactions. In a letter written from the National Palace in Mexico City, he estimated that as of late 1847, the United States had captured some 600 artillery pieces.[56]

U.S. aid to the regime in Mexico City included more than the transfer of weapons to the Mexican army. The occupiers also sought to revive internal commerce by regularly providing escorts for merchants seeking to reestablish the two main internal trade routes. They invited persons of commerce, both Mexican and foreign-born, to join escorted convoys traveling between Veracruz and Mexico City. This offer met with an enthusiastic response from traders and customers who transacted business along this key commercial route. For example, half of the 400 wagons in the convoy of April 16, 1848, belonged to Mexican merchants. The U.S. Army offered escorts on another key route as well. Any Mexican reaching Mazipil, Zacatecas, or Parras, Nuevo Léon, with gold or silver for sale received a military escort to Saltillo. From there, a new group of protectors escorted the convoys onward toward the coast.[57] Merchants traveling on less important journeys occasionally received protection, as well.[58] Almost all of the U.S. escorts served on the Mexico City–Veracruz route and the roads from the main mining districts of the north. The United States provided these services because its national interest dictated it do so.

As Polk previously acknowledged, his country could not obtain a lasting peace without the existence of a stable México. For the United States, the decision to sign a treaty and an armistice providing various types of support to the Mexican government in return for that regime's agreement to cede the northern provinces represented the most palatable of a number of unpleasant alternatives. A review of those other courses of action demonstrates the point.

Contrary to General Taylor's suggestion, Polk could not unilaterally withdraw. To do so would remove a major incentive for Mexican nationalists to support the treaty. As long as the U.S. Army remained an occupier, Polk could offer to leave that territory he conceded to be Mexican if

México agreed to surrender land that the United States wanted. But, if the United States unilaterally withdrew, he would have no such inducement to offer México. Also, a unilateral withdrawal would deny the United States' conquest the finality and legitimacy that can be conveyed only by a treaty of peace. Finally, Polk believed that regrouping at the Rio Grande would not bring peace. "To retire to a line, and simply hold and defend it, would not terminate the war. On the contrary, it would encourage México to persevere, and tend to protract it indefinitely," Polk asserted.[59] Thus ended General Taylor's hope that such a course of action would be pursued.

The alternate choice of annexing all of México held no attraction for the Polk administration. Looking back upon his experiences as general-in-chief, Scott concluded that the most likely result of annexation or military occupation would be "that all México, or rather the active part thereof, would again relapse into a permanent state of revolution, being with one against annexation."[60] Given his unsuccessful experience in controlling Mexican guerrillas in the comparatively small arena of the Veracruz–Mexico City supply corridor, Scott possessed little desire to try a similar experiment across the entire nation. During the ten-month period from his landing at Collado Beach to his departure from México, Scott sought to end the guerrilla threat to his supply lines by a variety of means. He began by assigning massive escorts to each convoy, then decreed collective fiscal penalties against communities en route, and subsequently sanctioned the widespread burning of ranches and pueblos. When those steps failed, Scott established fixed posts manned by thousands of troops from Veracruz to Mexico City and ordered the summary execution of captured guerrillas. None of these measures succeeded. The January 1848 convoy attacks proved as much. The major threat that partisans posed to the U.S. supply lines ended only when the Mexican government ordered these attacks to cease.

Like Scott's, Taylor's forces also were unable to control the mobile Mexican cavalry operating against his troops. By early 1847, the cavalry of Generals José Vicente Miñón and José Lopez Urrea dominated the northern Mexican countryside between Tampico and Saltillo.[61] Since that time, the prospect of a general uprising had figured prominently in Taylor's considerations. It was in this context of continuing anti-U.S. sentiments, increased peasant rebellion, and political destabilization that Taylor had suggested a unilateral withdrawal to the Rio Grande. He argued that a force of 10,000 cavalry based along that line would be able to defend the newly conquered territory from Mexican attacks. But his commander-in-chief considered that to be a self-defeating option.

Both Taylor and Scott clearly understood that even as late as 1848, many Mexicans could summon the will and the capacity to fight additional battles if sufficiently provoked. The clash of March 16, 1848, at Santa Cruz de Rosales, Chihuahua, proved the validity of their assumption. The chain of events leading to this confrontation began when Colonel Sterling Price led a force south from Santa Fe, New Mexico, on February 8, 1848.[62] He sought to capture the Chihuahuan capital and later justified his expedition on the grounds that, at the time, he did not know about the Treaty of Guadalupe Hidalgo. On March 7, he took Chihuahua City. However, the state's governor, General Ángel Álvarez Trias, proved himself as tenacious a warrior as his uncle, Juan Álvarez. When Price continued his advance south with a force of 900 men and twelve artillery pieces, Trias regrouped to block the advancing force at Santa Cruz de Rosales. When the two armies met, the Mexican commander requested and received two truces. During these periods, he told Price of the treaty. Price did not believe him.

As a result, on March 16, 1848, U.S. forces began a bombardment of Trias' men, who by then had fortified the villa. According to Mexican historian José María Roa Barcena, 900 of his countrymen supported by eleven artillery pieces repulsed the first attack, causing Price's men to abandon their position and some of their artillery.[63] However, Cadmus Wilcox, a U.S. historian of the same battle, maintained that the attacking troops did not abandon their artillery following this first assault and that the Mexican force amounted to no more than 700 men.[64] Both scholars agree that the Mexicans repulsed the first attack. Price's men returned to their original positions in mid-afternoon and struck again. This time, they succeeded in seizing the villa, General Trias, and forty-two of his aides before night. The U.S. commander found the tenacity and skill of the Mexicans so impressive that he returned their officers' swords.[65]

Although the Battle of Santa Cruz de Rosales ended in a tactical triumph for the United States, the victory had dire strategic implications. By most criteria, Chihuahua held no potential for resistance. In 1847, U.S. forces under Colonel Alexander William Doniphan had successfully invaded the state, winning a February 28 victory at Sacramento. By early 1848, Chihuahua's government possessed no source of revenue other than its monopoly on tobacco and could not expect any support from a national government incapable of controlling even the states adjacent to the federal capital. In spite of such dire circumstances, Chihuahuans raised an army that first fought Price at the state capital, retreated intact, and then fought again with valor and persistence at Santa Cruz de Rosales. These Mexicans conclusively demonstrated that the capacity for serious continued resistance to the U.S. Army existed at an autonomous regional level. More importantly, the Chihuahuans proved that this potential hostility would become a violent reality if the nation's civilians felt provoked.

The prospect of the Mexican people acting as had the Chihuahuans at Santa Cruz de Rosales held grim implications for the United States. Chihuahua constituted a mere 2.1 percent of México's population of 7,016,300.[66] From that small demographic base, these northerners raised a force of at least 700 men to fight Price's advance. A similarly successful recruiting effort among the entire nation's population would have yielded a force of 33,274 volunteers.[67] That total far exceeds the number of men that the *Plaza Mayor* (headquarters staff) of the Mexican army cited as necessary to continue the fighting. The Battle of Santa Cruz de Rosales proved that the potential for substantial armed resistance to the continued occupation of additional Mexican territory clearly existed at the state level.

These events in Chihuahua also confirmed an aspect of the war's military history previously acknowledged by Smith and conceded by Commodore Perry: "The Mexicans are not deficient in personal courage, nothing is wanting to make them good soldiers, other than military discipline and national ardor which cannot be expected of men impressed as they are into service, in the most cruel and ruthless manner."[68] Many encounters during the war confirm the truth of Perry's statement. In the course of the battles fought in the Valley of México, a New York regiment suffered 90 percent casualties.[69] When properly motivated and led, Mexicans proved themselves capable of formidable resistance. By mid-1848, the national state no longer commanded such allegiance. Scott understood quite clearly that given the provocation of continued occupation or annexation, Mexicans would resist. Many U.S. civilians, including powerful congressional factions, also resisted the idea of continued occupation or annexation.

The most influential opponent of the latter course was Senator John C. Calhoun of South Carolina. He led the powerful southern faction of senators in defense of that region's autonomy and its system of slave labor.[70]

Because both Calhoun and his supporters belonged to the same party as the president, their withdrawal of support left annexationists in the Polk administration with only a part of their fellow Democrats behind them in the face of a united Whig opposition. These southerners voiced two objections to annexation. As Calhoun correctly stated, the Mexicans remained "a people hostile to slavery," and their annexation to the Union would "erect a perpetual bar to its [slavery's] extension."[71] Also, the addition of seven million new citizens opposed to the South's peculiar institution also would have irreparably turned the balance of power in Congress against the South.

Cultural considerations also represented a further impediment to the addition of millions of Mexicans to the U.S. electorate. Senator Daniel Webster of Massachusetts asserted, "I am not sure that it is best for everyone to receive our forms. . . .You cannot make free men of persons unaccustomed to self government."[72] Webster proposed that the United States seek only the territory claimed by the former Republic of Texas. That boundary would have fixed the southern and western borders of his nation at the Rio Grande. In addition to that publicly stated concern, Webster and his fellow New Englanders also understood that each new territory added to the new union meant a further increase in the number of western senators and a consequent diminution of their region's influence.

Some opponents of annexation spoke in racially charged terms. For example, Senator John M. Clayton of Delaware argued that Mexicans came from "a race totally different from ourselves," and that they could never assimilate. Congressman Jacob Collamer of Vermont claimed, "[W]e should destroy our nationality by such an act [annexation]. We shall cease to be the people that we were; we cease to be Saxon Americanized."[73] Invariably, a question arises as to whether or not the belief of many North

Americans in their own racial superiority constituted a more important factor in the U.S. desire to withdraw than did the military realities. Here, precise distinctions remain a necessity. The annexation proposals against which Calhoun and the Whigs most strongly propounded their racial and culturally based arguments were those that called for the absorption of all of México into the United States. That outcome would have added approximately 7,016,300 Mexicans to the U.S. population with profound implications for the inhabitants of both polities. By contrast, the disputes within the Polk administration focused not upon seizing all of México, but upon the permanent conquest of the most sparsely populated areas.

Expansionists such as Polk, Buchanan, and Secretary of the Treasury Robert Walker sought that part of México north of the twenty-sixth parallel. Within that territory lived only a small fraction all Mexicans. The specifics are as follows:

TABLE 5.1
MEXICAN TERRITORY SOUGHT BY PRESIDENT POLK

State	Population	Percent of Mexican population	Mexican population as percent of non-slave U.S. population
The Californias	33,439	0.48%	0.30%
Nuevo México	57,026	0.81%	0.52%
Chihuahua	147,600	2.10%	1.34%
Coahuila	75,340	1.07%	0.68%
Nuevo León	86,108	1.22%	0.78% i
Sonora	124,000	1.77%	1.13%
TOTAL	523,521	7.45%	4.76% ii

i The figure for Nuevo León excludes the estimated population of the city of Monterrey, which lies south of the twenty-sixth parallel.

ii Mexican population is taken from Table 2.1. The U.S. population for the national census taken prior to the war is from Executive Document 263, 1840 Census, microfilm roll T-825, NARA, Washington, D.C.

Since state boundaries do not precisely coincide with the twenty-sixth parallel, the total figure is not exact. For example, all of Coahuila's population is included even though a part of that state lies south of the designated meridian. Similarly, the small portion of Sinaloa north of that line is not listed above. The total figure of 523,521 should be accurate to within 5 percent.

Polk's diary indicates that at no time during the war did he or Secretary of State James Buchanan consider annexing all of México. Their disputes concerned whether or not to confine their permanent conquests to the Californias and Nuevo México or to include all of the territory north of the twenty-sixth parallel. The first option increased the population of the United States by 0.82 percent while the latter choice would have increased that number by 4.76 percent. The addition of either number of Mexicans did not imply a major change in the nation's demographic profile. The senators and congressmen often cited by historians addressed the radically different proposal of total annexation rather than the more demographically modest one Polk considered.

Also, many of the Whigs in Congress joined Webster in opposing the annexation of any new territory beyond the Texas boundary. Their power proved to be so considerable that, in early 1848, they passed a House resolution accusing Polk of having dishonestly presented the facts of the first clash between the armed forces in an effort to coax a declaration of war from the Congress.

Thus, the Polk administration's concerns included political opposition within the United States, the certainty of renewed guerrilla attacks if the U.S. Army remained in México, the political destabilization of the Mexican regime resulting from the growing waves of campesino assaults, the probability of U.S. involvement in that intra-Mexican war should his army remain in México, and the prospect of additional battles such as the one fought at Santa Cruz de Rosales. Finally, the U.S. Congress' continued refusal to provide the army with adequate supplies created an additional crisis. Scott summarized his forces' situation February 28, 1848, in a report in which he reminded his superior "that the chief commissary (Captain Grayson) of this army has not received a dollar from the United States, since we landed at Vera Cruz [*sic*], March 9."[74] The general-in-chief then catalogued some of the consequences, including a lack of blankets, coats, and shoes. To provide his army with such minimal requirements, Scott manufactured these items in Veracruz.[75]

The president himself held no doubt that in certain circumstances, the Congress would end its financial support of the armed forces. In describing the probable consequences of rejecting the treaty negotiated by his ambassador, Nicholas Philip Trist, in favor an alternative pact annexing more Mexican territory, Polk wrote: "A majority of one branch of Congress is opposed to my administration; they have falsely charged that the war was brought on and is continued by me with a view to the conquest of México; and if I were to reject a treaty made upon my own terms, as authorized in April last, with the unanimous approval of the Cabinet, the probability is that Congress would not grant either men or money to prosecute the war. Should this be the result, the army now in México would be constantly wasting and diminishing in number, and I might at last be compelled to withdraw them and thus lose the two Provinces of New México and Upper California, which were ceded to the United States by this treaty."[76]

Polk's fear of a congressionally administered defeat in the form of a termination of army funding and Scott's message about the state of his supplies reflected the partial success of the Jeffersonian Democrat, Albert Gallatin. A former secretary of the treasury, Gallatin emerged as one of the most powerful opponents of the war: "There is no efficient constitutional power by which he [Polk] can be checked but that of withholding supplies necessary to the extent of effecting the intended purpose."[77] In light of these circumstances, the president's willingness to abandon his prior preference for a new international boundary drawn at the twenty-sixth parallel becomes quite explicable. He now accepted a border drawn at the

Rio Grande. Sonora, Chihuahua, Coahuila, and Nuevo León would remain Mexican. As detachments of the U.S. cavalry and infantry and artillery began boarding the transports at Veracruz for the northward journey home, Mexicans in arms still confronted each other.

First among these stood the indigenously based partisan groups. Although their rebellions in the Huasteca and indeed throughout central México took place in many pueblos, these combatants did not coordinate their attacks on a regional or national basis. By failing to do so, they rendered themselves far weaker than they might have been. By contrast, the Yucatecan guerrillas coordinated their actions over the length and breadth of the entire peninsula, thereby posing a far greater challenge to the national government.[78]

Simultaneously, General Mariano Paredes raised the standard of revolt but did so from the opposite end of the socio-economic and political spectrum of Mexican society. He stood as a champion of the most conservative criollo factions. In 1841, he had been one of the leaders of the military junta that issued the centralist and reactionary laws known as the Bases de Tacubaya. In January 1846, he had led a successful coup against the federal government, which he accused of trying to sell California and Texas to the United States. Paredes had nominated one of the nation's harshest opponents of peasant rebellions as vice president—General Nicolas Bravo—and he actively sought to advance the monarchist cause.[79] In 1848, Paredes declared the Treaty of Guadalupe Hidalgo a betrayal of the nation and called for war upon the moderate Mexican government that had signed the pact.

The government in Mexico City, strengthened by the armaments received from its recent foe, continued the bloody task of reestablishing its authority. By August 11, 1848, Álvarez confidently reported that with a force of 1,000 troops "well armed and equipped," he saved the Sultepec and Zacualtipán areas of México state from "the scandalous movements in the pueblos that exist to incite odious, bloody, and barbarous war of the castes."[80] Rebellions in other parts of México also earned sharp attacks from the national state. In late 1848, General Anastasio Bustamante entered the Sierra Gorda to practice again his time-tested skills of crushing revolts. He led a force of 1,200 national guardsmen and approximately 1,100 veterans.[81] On the northern frontier, a force of 3,428 soldiers sought to control hostile forces identified as barbarians, Apaches, and Comanches.[82] In January 1849, the minister of war and marine described the regime's success in central México: "In the pueblos of the Huasteca, the state of México, and to the coast of Puebla, the war of castes also appeared. The government used force, the subversives suffered various defeats, and the government granted pardons to the rest using faculties invested in the national executive, to achieve the end of these disastrous revolutions, reducing many ringleaders and a multitude of Indígenas to obedience of the laws."[83]

By contrast, Mayan rebels of the Yucatán proved far more difficult to control. As of December 13, 1848, the federal government deployed 16,000 of its 21,278 troops against the Maya, with the remaining 5,278 fighting in other areas of the nation. In addition, the various reconstituted national guard units, whose strength totaled 24,973 men by February 1849, remained ready to suppress rebellions occurring within the individual states."[84] As measured by the commitment of troops, the common inhabitants of the nation were perceived as a more potent enemy of México than the invader who had seized half of the country's territory. Much bitter fighting lay ahead, but the elitist regime would triumph against its internal foes.

CHAPTER SIX

CONCLUSION

Don't worry John. The history books will clean it up.

BENJAMIN FRANKLIN TO JOHN ADAMS

Inevitably, we attach meanings to the great events of our lives. While individuals often transform those memories into writing, nations build monuments to their chosen and shared recollections. México's most prominent commemoration of the war begins several yards beyond the point at which the twelve lanes of Mexico City's Paseo de la Reforma turn west into Chapultepec Park. There, visitors pass through a tall, imposing wrought iron gate and walk down a straight stone esplanade more than sixty feet wide that reaches the Altar de la Patria. In front of a massive curved marble wall stands a statue of two grim-visaged figures. The first, a woman with hair braided in an indígena manner, stares into the distance. Beside her, a statute of a young, athletic man looks over the visitor. The metaphorical representation is a mature *patria* and a young *nación* focusing beyond the scene of immense tragedy. Overall, the effect is sobering.

North of the Rio Grande, the most noted commemoration of the war is not a great monument, but Carlos Nebel's painting entitled *General Scott's Entrance into Mexico City*.[1] (See page 113.) On the left side of the canvas, serried ranks of cavalry stand at attention in front of the national cathedral. In the upper portion of the picture, an oversized U.S. flag flies from the roof of the National Palace. In the foreground, Scott and a party of his senior officers, all mounted and resplendent in dress uniform, survey the scene. Nebel's painting implies a definitive and victorious conclusion. That implication and many additional widely held assumptions about this war are false.

Perhaps the greatest such myth is the contention that only one war took place from 1846 to 1848. In reality, both the partisan struggle waged against the U.S. Army and the guerrilla revolt launched against the elitist regime changed the course of history. The breadth and ferocity of the ethnically and economically based campesino uprising compelled the

Sculptor Ernesto Tamariz's monumental work honors those who fell in Mexico's defense. Like the painting of Scott's entrance into Mexico City, less tidy realities remain unseen.
Ernesto Tamariz, Altar de la patria. Chapultepec Park, Mexico City.

One war ends — General Winfield Scott reviews his victorious troops after the fall of Mexico City — the other wars continued.
Carlos Nebel, *General Scott's Entrance into Mexico City on 14 September 1847*, 1851, Oil on canvas, Museo Nacional de las Intervenciones. Reproducción Autorizada por el Instituto Nacional de Antropología e Historia.

Mexican elite to abandon considerations of future resistance to the United States and to refocus military efforts upon restoring their own hegemony. Partisan warfare also altered the United States' priorities and attitudes. The guerrilla struggle against the U.S. Army along the Veracruz–Mexico City corridor and in the northern part of the country proved to both Scott and Taylor that continued occupation would be a difficult and bloody task. The Chihuahuans who defended Santa Cruz de Rosales demonstrated that ordinary Mexicans who had not yet become warriors would fight if provoked.

The most powerful arguments for assigning such great importance to the partisan movements flow not only from field reports, but also from the evidence provided by the highest-ranking officials of both national governments. In the case of the guerrillas fighting the Mexican government, Minister of War and Marine Luis de la Rosa acknowledged that, by the end of 1848, the Mexican state was setting more soldiers against other Mexicans than the national army deployed against the foreign invaders during the 1847 campaign in the Valley of México.[2] That level of fighting represented not disorder or anarchy, but civil war. In the case of the partisan resistance to the U.S. Army, General-in-Chief Winfield Scott bluntly told his superiors that an indefinite occupation would result in the coalescence of a national resistance movement (no doubt led by the light corps that he signally failed to eliminate). General Zachary Taylor acknowledged his own failure to destroy the partisan forces in northern México and concluded that a unilateral withdrawal to the Rio Grande–Alta California boundary would be the wisest course.

The persistence and deadliness with which the guerrillas fought the U.S. Army diminished the conqueror's territorial ambitions. In 1846, high-ranking officials such as Secretary of State James Buchanan considered the twenty-sixth parallel to be the appropriate post-war boundary. North of that line lay not only the lands that would be included in the states of Arizona, California, Nevada, New Mexico, and Utah, but all of Chihuahua and Sonora as well as major portions of Baja California, Coahuila, Tamaulipas, and Nuevo León. During the covert May–June 1847 peace negotiations undertaken by U.S. negotiator Moses Y. Beach, the Mexicans with whom he spoke learned that a boundary at the twenty-sixth parallel remained the Polk administration's goal.[3] But, by November 1847, President Polk had reduced those demands by more than 187,000 square miles. He abandoned his quest for any territory in the present-day Mexican states of Chihuahua, Sonora, Coahuila, Tamaulipas, Nuevo León, or Baja California.[4] The following map illustrates this point: By virtue of their sacrifices, the unconquered light corps and its counterparts in northern México ensured that this territory remained Mexican.

In slighting the importance of the partisans, both Mexicans and Americans of that time served their own interests. To provide a cloak of legitimacy for the decision to surrender almost half of the nation's territory, prominent Mexicans such as Manuel de la Peña y Peña argued that the only alternatives were surrender or anarchy. By contrast, Manuel Crescencio Rejon, a Puro liberal member of the federal chamber of deputies, argued that the treaty would bring not peace, but "the political death of the Republic."[5] He contended that once the new frontier came into being, the United States would repeat the previous pattern of illegally establishing an economic presence on the Mexican side of the border and then initiating the types of conduct that led to the outbreak of war in 1846.[6] His fellow deputy, Benito Juárez, also denounced the Treaty of Guadalupe Hidalgo and urged that it be rejected.

In 1862, Juárez spoke to México's federal legislators on a similar occasion: Just fourteen years after the Treaty of Guadalupe Hidalgo, the French army prepared to march into Mexico City as Scott's forces had done in 1848. Yet unlike Peña y Peña, he did not argue that only surrender or anarchy awaited his nation. Speaking to the legislators just prior to leading his defeated forces north to the border city that today bears his name, Juárez told them, "Adversity, Citizen-Deputies, dismays only contemptible people, and our people are ennobled by great deeds."[7] In 1848, México's national leadership indeed deserved such an appellation, as does any government that seeks to surrender to an invader to accelerate the efficacy with which it might wage war upon its own people. Understandably, Peña y Peña did not dwell on the long-standing causes that led so many Mexicans to rebel against the national regime. The former president of México and justice of its supreme court did not stand alone in his efforts to reconstruct history.

Alternate outcomes: The boundary sought by expansionists such as Secretary of State James Buchanan dissolved in the face of Mexican resisstance and U.S. Ambassador Nicholes P. Trist's consequent negotiation. Senator Daniel Webster's frontier on the Rio Grande proved too llittle for his countrymen's appetites.

Map adapted from Plate 115 of The Times Atlas of the World Comprehensive Edition
© Collins Bartholomew Ltd 1975.

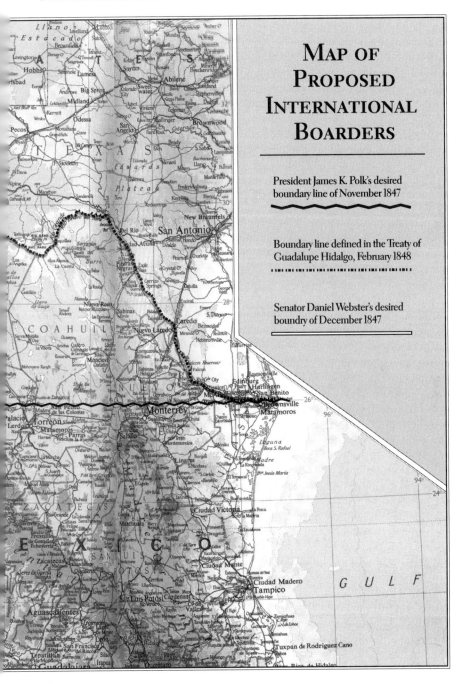

MAP OF PROPOSED INTERNATIONAL BOARDERS

President James K. Polk's desired boundary line of November 1847

Boundary line defined in the Treaty of Guadalupe Hidalgo, February 1848

Senator Daniel Webster's desired boundry of December 1847

Colonel Ethan Allen Hitchcock also slighted the partisans, implicitly denying that the guerrillas of late 1847 and 1848 even constituted a military force. After writing that the general-in-chief wanted to be relieved of command "about Nov 2 [1847]—when he supposed active military operations would cease in this country," Hitchcock asserted, "they ceased in fact in September, on the entrance of the United States Army into the city on the 14th of September."[8] Yet U.S. military operations in México did not end on that day. To the contrary, Scott's subsequent dispatch of 21 percent of his force to fixed points along the logistical artery running from Veracruz to Mexico City, his orders that these units actively patrol in an effort to engage the guerrillas, the efforts of General Lane's mounted column to hunt down light corps forces, and the order that all guerrillas be shot clearly prove that the fighting continued well past September 1847. The partisan attacks launched during January 1848 further contradict Hitchcock's assertion that military operations ended in September of the previous year.

Hitchcock's decision to place the guerrillas beyond the borders of consideration may well account for discrepancies in the U.S. casualty figures for the war. As noted in Appendix A, very detailed research efforts confirm that official records cannot account for the disappearance of about 2,800 of those soldiers. Many of those unexplained casualties might well have occurred fighting a force that Chief of Intelligence Hitchcock refused to acknowledge. In consigning the guerrillas to the periphery of history, he and several generations of U.S. historians sustained the comforting impressions conveyed by Nebel's painting. Only on that canvas and in Hitchcock's diary did the U.S. triumph appear complete.

Another guerrilla uprising, one that targeted the Mexican elite, also challenged accepted images. For different reasons, the ideologically motivated among the ranks of both the right and the left often portrayed México's peasants and indigenous citizens as people acted upon rather than as those who acted of their own volition. The framework of both the liberals who deemed them in need of uplift and reform as well as of the conservatives who branded these most Mexican of Mexicans as backward and uncomprehending cannot be reconciled with the events of 1846–48. During those years, the rural rebels quite clearly understood the effect that the war with the United States had upon the repressive powers of the Mexican state, and the repeated demand for the restoration of their land confirmed that they did indeed have a specific objective. As John H. Coatsworth pointed out, México's peasants have "a unique history of precocious politicization and assertiveness beginning in the early nineteenth century."[9] Their actions during the México–United States war support his judgment.

For a brief period starting in April 1846 and ending in August 1848, the United States altered the balance of power between the two great contending forces within México. On one side stood the western ideal with its emphasis upon individual land tenure, nuclear families, global markets, urban aggregations, and a hierarchical society structured on the basis of wealth and ancestry. The contrasting Mesoamerican world valued the communal life of the pueblo, the extended family, the local and regional market, and local autonomy. When the U.S. Army altered the balance between those two forces, rebellion flourished.

Future U.S. interventions in México would follow the 1848 practice of aiding national elites to achieve desired objectives rather than the 1847 tactic of overt invasion. In the latter year, the rulers of México stood ready to cede territory to the United States in return for various types of assistance that would facilitate the reestablishment of their own hegemony. Polk responded positively. This strategy succeeded in 1848 and again during the Mexican Revolution. In 1914, the United States provided the constitutionalist forces of Venustiano Carranza with machine guns, modern cannon, barbed wire, munitions, and training in the contest against the forces of Francisco "Pancho" Villa. The 1846–48 war marked the emergence of this tactic. In the more than 150 years that mark the space between the end of that conflict and the present, the United States has also provided weapons, munitions, and training to other Latin American governments. In Brazil, Bolivia, Colombia, Chile, Cuba, the Dominican Republic, El Salvador, Haiti, Nicaragua, Panama, and Venezuela, national regimes received military assistance to fight domestic rebels hostile to the interests of the United States. Thus, the precedent set by the 1848 transfer of arms in Mexico City evolved into a standard U.S. policy.

Similarly, the peasantry continued its own resistance, persevering in its attachment to the land during the dispossessions of the Porfiriato to rise yet again in the Mexican Revolution and reclaim that which once had been theirs. Inevitably, belief in lengthy and powerful historical themes such as the conflict between the western and the indigenous Méxicos breeds a deep skepticism toward claims that historical transformations can occur with ease and rapidity. The contention that commercial accords such as the North American Free Trade Agreement can alter these centuries-long divisions within México represents one such argument. In reality, the economic polarization of present-day México and the migration of millions of displaced rural residents fleeing to overcrowded cities and across the northern border bring to mind the Porfiriato. Then, as now, so many Mexicans lost the land that stood at the center of their existence.

However, during the 1846–48 war, military and civilian leaders in each nation flattered themselves with the belief that their actions could determine the course of history. To some extent, this may have been the case. Both Taylor and some Mexican officials believed that at the Battle of Buena Vista, Santa Anna's decision to launch his numerically superior force piecemeal, rather than en masse, enabled the U.S. Army to win that clash and remain in northern México. Similarly, the fact that just one of the U.S. Army's generals in the field, Joseph Lane, understood that guerrillas only could be fought by columns as mobile as their own, rendered life easier for some partisans.

In another sense, the long course of history preordained the denouement of this conflict. The aching decades and centuries of abuse heaped upon the vast majority of Mexicans by their rulers set the stage for a massive uprising as soon as an invader weakened the national army. Similarly, the expansionist worldview that stood at the center of American consciousness ensured war with those who blocked the westward sweep to the Pacific. Perhaps the final truth remains that while humans may flatter themselves with the notion that they are masters of their own fates and the captains of their own ships, they sail upon a very great sea whose limits extend far beyond the horizon.

THE RANKS
OF THE DEAD

The number of deaths suffered by the U.S. Army in action against partisans cannot be precisely determined. Several reasons account for this. First, statistics compiled by staff of that era are imprecise. Soon after the war ended, Edward D. Mansfield, a historian of the conflict, extensively reviewed available records[1]. He broke the statistics down into categories of those U.S. soldiers killed from the start of the war to the final full month of combat (January 1848) and those who died thereafter:

TABLE A.1
UNITED STATES LOSSES IN THE 1846–48 WAR

A. From April 1846 to January 1848

Killed in action or died from wounds up to January 1848	1,556
Died due to disease up to January 1848	5,987
Discharged for disability up to 1848	5,432
Desertions up to January 1848	4,925
Subtotal	17,900

B. From January 1848 through July 1848

Deaths resulting from combat and disease plus discharges and desertions	4,500
C. Combination of itemized losses	22,400
D. Total reported losses	25,200
E. Number of soldiers unaccounted for (D minus C)	2,800

Mansfield cannot account for the discrepancy of 2,800 personnel. We may assume that many of these men fell to partisan attacks. Primary source documents of this conflict evidence a disposition on the part of senior officers to slight or even ignore partisan forces. The most glaring example is the previously cited decision of the chief of intelligence, Colonel Ethan Allen Hitchcock, to assert that the dispatch of thousands of troops to counter-guerrilla postings did not constitute a military operation. Similarly, Major Folliot Lally's statement that he merely restored order without reference to any tally of injured and killed on either side illustrates another sort of incomplete report.

Consequently, we are left only with the testimony of field officers and infantry who conveyed respect for the abilities of the partisans they faced along the Veracruz–Mexico City corridor.

INTRODUCTION

1. Minutes, January 18, 1848, continuation of January 5 meeting of the municipal council of the city of Toluca, box 5, folder 26, Archivo Histórico Municipal de Toluca de Lerdo, Toluca, México.
2. In this text, the terms "partisan" and "guerrilla" are used interchangeably.

CHAPTER 1

The epigraph comes from Guillermo Bonfil Batalla, *México Profundo: Reclaiming a Civilization*, trans. Philip A. Dennis (Austin: University of Texas Press, 1996), xviii.

1. William M. Denevan, ed., *The Native Population of the Americas in 1492* (Madison: University of Wisconsin Press, 1976), 291; Woodrow Borah and Sherburne F. Cook, "The Aboriginal Population of Central Mexico on the Eve of the Spanish Conquest," *Ibero-Americana* 45 (1963): 88–90. Although historians Woodrow Borah and Sherburne F. Cook defend a higher population estimate of 25,400,000, the continuously disputed veracity of their figures is such that accepting Denevan's more prudent figure remains a desirable choice. As used herein, central México includes all of the territory of the present-day states of Colima, Guerrero, Hidalgo, Jalisco, México, Michoacán, Morelos, Nayarit, Oaxaca, Puebla, Tlaxcala, and Veracruz as well as parts of the states of Guanajuato, Querétaro, and Zacatecas.
2. Timothy E. Anna, *The Fall of the Royal Government in Mexico City* (Lincoln: University of Nebraska Press, 1978), 6.
3. Fernando (Hernán) Cortés, *Letters from Mexico* (New York: Grossman, 1971), 105, 108.
4. Charles Gibson, *The Aztecs Under Spanish Rule: A History of the Indians of the Valley of México, 1519–1810* (Palo Alto: Stanford University Press, 1964), 403–404.
5. Ibid., 406–407.
6. Lewis Hanke, *Aristotle and the American Indians: A Study in Race Prejudice in the Modern World* (Chicago: Henry Regnery Company, 1959), 47.
7. Ibid.
8. Strictly speaking, an *encomienda* consisted of a grant issued by the colonial government that entitled its possessor to commandeer the labor of designated indigenous people. In return, the holder of the encomiendas bore an obligation to provide his charges with sustenance and spiritual guidance. Such obligations were far more frequently ignored than observed. Bartolome de la Casas, *A Short Account of the Destruction of the Indies* (London: Penguin Books, 1992).
9. Smuggling provides an illustrative example. Since mercantilist laws severely limited the importation of overseas products, the smuggling of such wares developed into a popular and lucrative practice.

10. Guillermo Bonfil Batalla discussed the development of this sort of patriotism in *México Profundo*, 95–96. This interpretation also is found in general texts such as Michael C. Meyer and William L. Sherman, *The Course of Mexican History* (New York: Oxford University Press, 1995), 275–76.

11. Enrique Florescano, *Memory, Myth, and Time in México: From the Aztecs to Independence* (Austin: University of Texas Press, 1994), 184. Florescano contrasted this situation with that of the pre-conquest period, in which "the protagonist was a people or ethnic group united by one language, one origin, and one territory."

12. Lucas Alamán, *Historia de México* (Mexico City: Editoria Jus, 1942), 1: 403–404.

13. For a lengthier explanation of this interpretation of the end of México's war for independence, please refer to John Lynch, *The Spanish-American Revolutions, 1808–1826* (New York: W. W. Norton & Company, 1973), 319–33. The best history of those Mexicans who joined in writing the Constitution of Cadiz remains Nettie Lee Benson, *The Provincial Deputation in Mexico* (Austin: University of Texas Press, 1955).

14. José María Luis Mora, *Ensayos, ideas, y retratos* (Mexico City: Universidad Nacional Autonoma de México, 1941), 17.

15. Ibid., 159.

16. Ibid.

17. Waddy Thompson, *Recollections of México* (New York: Wiley and Putnam, 1846), 12.

18. Ibid., 150. Since a league's traditional measure is three miles, Thompson's statement means that such properties ranged in size from 720 to 900 square miles.

19. Excerpts from *El diario del gobierno*, July 22, 1838, and September 2, 1835, are in Michael Costeloe's essay entitled, "Hombres de bien in the age of Santa Anna," in Jaime E. Rodriguez O, ed., *Mexico in the Age of Democratic Revolutions* (Boulder: Lynne Reiner Publishers, Inc., 1994), 252–53.

20. Ibid., 247.

21. A different school of thought holds that the ascension of liberals to some of México's highest offices and the Constitution of 1824 prove that the 1821–46 period was not dominated by a criollo oligarchy. Also, a recent work by Richard A. Warren, *Vagrants and Citizens: Politics and the Masses in Mexico City from Colony to Republic* (Wilmington, Del.: SR Books, 2001), argues that suffrage indeed did become more common in some precincts of Mexico City. However, the preponderance of evidence favors the contrary position taken by Costeloe.

22. A brief and concise description of Alamán's position can be found in John Lynch, *Caudillos in Spanish America, 1800–1850* (Oxford: Clarendon Press, 1992), 419.

23. Republic of México, Bases generales, Ministro de relaciones exterior, gobernativo y policia, 27 January 1847, box 319, file 3, sheet 1, sin sección, Ramo Gobernación, Archivo General de la Nación, Mexico City, D.F.

24. Among the more noteworthy histories of such rebellions are Peter F. Guardino, *Peasants, Politics, and the Formation of México's National State: Guerrero, 1800–1857* (Palo Alto: Stanford University Press, 1996) and Leticia Reina, *Las rebeliones campesinas en México, 1819–1906* (Mexico City: Siglo Veintiuno, 1980).

25. This description of the Álvarez Rebellion encapsulates an essay by John Mason Hart, "The 1840s Southwestern Mexico Peasants' War: Conflict in a Transitional Society," in *Riot, Rebellion, and Revolution*, ed. Friedrich Katz (Princeton: Princeton University Press, 1988), 249–68.

26. Will Fowler, "Civil Conflict in Independent Mexico, 1821–1857: An Overview," in *Rumours of War: Civil Conflict in Nineteenth-Century Latin America*, ed. Rebecca Earle (London: Institute of Latin American Studies, 2000), 49–86.

27. Ibid., 267.

CHAPTER 2

1. James K. Polk, *The Diary of James K. Polk during His Presidency, 1845 to 1849*, ed. Milo Milton Quaife (Chicago: A. C. McClurg & Company, 1910), 400–401.

2. Manuel de la Peña y Peña, Algunos Documentos, 3–26, in Ward McAfee and J. Cordell Robinson, *Origins of the Mexican War: A Documentary Source Book* (Salisbury, N.C.: Documentary Publications, 1982), 1: 150–53.

3. David M. Pletcher, *The Diplomacy of Annexation: Texas, Oregon, and the Mexican War* (Columbia: University of Missouri Press, 1973), 441.

4. Winfield Scott, *Memoirs of Lieut.-General Scott, LL.D.* (New York: Sheldon & Company, 1864), 2: 442.

5. Antoine Henri Jomini, *Life of Napoleon*, trans. H. W. Halleck, LL.D. (New York: D. Van Nostrand, 1864), 1: 444–46.

6. Ibid., 446–47.

7. Ibid.

8. Polk, *Diary*, ed. Quaife, 409.

9. Zachary Taylor, *Letters of Zachary Taylor from the Battlefields of the Mexican War* (1908; Reprint, New York: Kraus Reprint Company, 1970), 183.

10. Ethan Allen Hitchcock, *Diary*, 26 December 1849, Box 2, 48: 2–3, Gilcrease Museum of Western History, Tulsa, Okla. General William Worth, a subordinate of General Taylor in the opening phases of the war, commanded a force in the assault on Monterrey. Subsequently, he transferred to Scott's command and played a key role in the campaign in central México, where he also served as military governor of Mexico City. Edward H. Moseley and Paul C. Clark, Jr., *Historical Atlas of the United States–Mexican War: Wars, Revolution, and Civil Unrest* (Lanham, Md.: Scarecrow Press, 1997), 310–11.

11. Timothy D. Johnson, *Winfield Scott: The Quest for Military Glory* (Lawrence: University of Kansas Press, 1998), 167.

12. Major General Winfield Scott, General Order No. 87, 1 April 1847, General Scott's Orders (41 ?), Orders and Special Orders, Headquarters of the Army, War with Mexico 1847–1848, Entry Number 134, Records Group 94, Records of the Adjutant General's Office, National Archives and Records Administration, Washington, D.C.

13. Scott, General Order No. 101, 9 April 1847, Orders and Special Orders, NARA I.

14. Joseph E. Chance, ed., *Mexico under Fire, Being the Diary of Samuel Ryan Curtis, 3rd Ohio Volunteer Regiment, during the American Military Occupation of Northern Mexico, 1846–1847* (Fort Worth: Texas Christian University Press, 1994), 20.

15. Scott, General Order No. 87, Orders and Special Orders, NARA I.

16. Major General Winfield Scott, Proclamation, Mexican War 1845–1850, Orders, 1845–1850,Volunteer Division, February 18, 1847–December 18, 1847, 21: 38, PI 17, Entry Number 134, Records Group 94, Records of the Adjutant General's Office, NARA I.

17. Scott, General Order No. 87, Orders and Special Orders, NARA I.

18. General Zachary Taylor, Order No. 9, Orders 1845–1848, Mexican War 1845–1850, 4: 12, Records Group 94, Records of the Adjutant General's Office, NARA I.

19. Colonel Thomas Childs, Order No. 2, 11 March 1848, Colonels Gorman and Childs, Commanding Officers, Department of Puebla, Orders 1845–1848, March–June 1848, Volume 13, Entry 134, Records Group 94, Records of the Adjutant General's Office, NARA I.

20. George B. McClellan, *The Mexican War Diary of General George B. McClellan*, ed. William Starr Myers (Princeton: Princeton University Press, 1917), 18–19. In subsequent years, Meade rose to the rank of major general and commanded the Union Army at the critical battle of Gettysburg.

21. Hitchcock, Diary, July 1848, Box 2, 51: 126–27, GMWH.

22. On October 7, 1846, General Gideon Pillow expressed "the satisfaction he feels at the strict discipline, good instruction, and soldierly bearing exhibited by both the officers and men of the 3rd Regiment of Tennessee Volunteers." General Gideon Pillow, General Order 37, 7 October 1846, August 1846–April 1847 Pillow's Brigade, 15: 1, Entry Number 134, Records Group 94, NARA I.

23. Paul Foos, *A Short, Offhand, Killing Affair: Soldiers and Social Conflict during the Mexican-American War* (Chapel Hill: University of North Carolina Press, 2002), 25.

24. For further information about the 1844 Philadelphia riot, see Michael Feldberg's *The Turbulent Era: Riot and Disorder in Jacksonian America* (New York: Oxford University Press, 1980), 7–13. For references to the Charlestown riot, see Dumas Malone and Basil Rauch, *Empire for Liberty: The Genesis and Growth of the United States of America* (New York: Appleton-Century Crofts, Inc. 1960), 1: 603–605. Information about similar events in New York City is provided by Paul A. Gilje, *The Road to Mobocracy: Popular Disorder in New York City, 1753–1834* (Chapel Hill: University of North Carolina Press, 1987), 138–42, 207.

25. Scott, *Memoirs*, 2: 428.

26. Edward D. Mansfield, *Life and Services of General Winfield Scott Including the Siege of Veracruz, the Battle of Cerro Gordo, and the Battles in the Valley of Mexico, to the Conclusion of Peace and His Return to the United States* (New York: A. S. Barnes & Company, 1852), 375–76.

27. Executive Documents Printed by Order of the Senate of the United States During the First Session of the Thirtieth Congress Begun and Held at the City of Washington, December 6, 1847, in Eight Volumes, 1: 228–29. (Washington, D.C.: Wendell and Van Benthysen, 1847). U.S. Army Military Institute, Carlisle, PA.

28. Ibid., 230.

29. José María Roa Barcena, *Recuerdos de la invasion norteamericana: 1846–1848* (Mexico City: Editorial Porrúa, 1993), 1: 301.

30. Ibid., 302.

31. John James Peck, *The Sign of the Eagle: A View of Mexico, 1830 to 1855* (San Diego: Union-Tribune Publishing Company, 1970), 78.

32. Robert Anderson, *An Artillery Officer in the Mexican War 1846–7: Letters of Robert Anderson, Captain 3rd Artillery, U.S.A.* (New York: G. P. Putnam's Sons, 1911), 91.

33. Jacob J. Oswandel, *Notes of the Mexican War 1846–1847–1848* (Philadelphia, 1885), 92–93.

34. Scott, *Memoirs*, 2: 429.

35. Ibid., 427.

36. Ibid., 421.

37. Francis Jennings, *The Founders of America: How Indians Discovered the Land, Pioneered in It, and Created a Great Classical Civilization; How They Were Plunged into a New Dark Age by Invasion and Conquest, and How They Are Reviving* (New York: W. W. Norton & Company, 1993), 333.

38. Chance, *Mexico under Fire*, 174.

39. Samuel L. Chamberlain, *My Confession: Recollections of a Rogue*, ed. William. H. Goetzmann (Austin: Texas State Historical Association, 1996), 193.

40. Ibid.

41. Major General Winfield Scott, General Order No. 129, 29 April 1847, Headquarters of the Army in Mexico, January–May 1847, Mexican War 1845–1850, Entry Number 134, Records Group 94, Records of the Adjutant General's Office, NARA 1.

42. This assertion is based upon a reading of all military reports from the 1846–48 war in the National Archives and Records Administration facilities in Washington, D.C., as well as upon a review of all pertinent records of the U.S. Army Military Institute, the Archivo General de la Nación, and the Archivo General de la Defensa Nacional.

43. Hitchcock, *Diary*, 20 April 1847, Box 2, Mandas (Museum object 3646.153), p. 1, GMWH.

44. Ibid.

45. John Reese Kenly, *Memoirs of a Maryland Volunteer: War with Mexico in the Years 1846–1848* (Philadelphia: J. B. Lippincott & Company, 1873), 370.

46. E. A. Hitchcock, Circular, 17 October 1847, General Correspondence May 9, 1847–December 10, 1847, Papers of E. A. Hitchcock, Manuscripts Division, Library of Congress, Washington, D.C.

47. José Fernando Ramírez, *Mexico during the War with the United States*, ed. Walter V. Scholes, trans. Elliot B. Scherr (Columbia: University of Missouri Press, 1950), 120.

48. Hitchcock, *Diary*, Box 2, 48: 89, GMWH.

49. Ibid.

50. Reglamento para el servicio de secciones ligera de la guardia nacional de los estados y territorios de la republica, folder XI.481.3/2586, p. 60, Archivo de la Defensa Nacional, Mexico City.

51. Ibid.

52. Paper, folder XI/481.3/2582, p. 3, ADN, Mexico City.

53. Two members of the lower clergy did obtain authorization to form guerrillas, but they were exceptions. Their patentes do not alter the fact that the federal government sought wealthy petitioners.

54. A Spaniard by birth, Padre Jarauta immigrated to México from Cuba and began his Mexican residence at the port of Veracruz in 1844. There, he served as military chaplain of the 2nd Infantry Regiment. *Diccionario porrúa de historia, biografia y geografiá de México* (Mexico City: Editorial Porrúa, 1995), 2: 1888. Another career officer receiving a commission, Mariano Arrillago Paredes, temporarily rendered loyalty service to the government before resuming his pre-war proclivity for rebellion. He helped lead the 1841 junta that imposed the conservative Bases de Tacubaya upon México. By conviction, he was a centralist monarchist. In 1848, he opposed the Treaty of Guadalupe Hidalgo. *Diccionario porrúa*, 3: 2637–38.

55. Captain Jack Hays, Texas Ranger, Section G220-XIV, p. 215, Justin H. Smith Collection, Diaries, Recollections, & Memoirs, Benson Latin American Collection, Austin, Tex.

CHAPTER 3

The epigraph from Philander Chase Johnson is cited in *The Oxford Dictionary of Quotations* 3rd ed. (New York: Oxford University Press, 1979), 273.

1. General Winfield Scott, letter to Brevet Colonel Henry Wilson, 13 April 1847. Executive Document 56 of the House of Representatives, *Messages from the President of the United States Transmitting Reports from the Secretary of State and the Secretary of War with Accompanying Documents in Compliance with the Resolution of the 7th February, 1848* (Washington, D.C.: Wendell and Van Benthuysen, 1848), 136.

2. Scott, letter to William Learned Marcy, 27 October 1847. Executive Document 56, 216–17.

3. Nathan Covington Brooks, *A Complete History of the Mexican War: Its Causes, Conduct, and Consequences* (Philadelphia: Grigg, Elliot & Company, 1849), 444–52.

4. José María Roa Barcena, *Recuerdos de la invasión norteamericana: 1846–1848* (Mexico City: Editorial Porrúa, 1971), 2: 107–108.

5. Emilio del Castillo Negrete, *Invasión de los norte-americanos* (Mexico City: Imprenta del Editor, 1890), 3: 450–54.

6. Scott, letter to Marcy, 27 October 1847. Executive Document 56, 216–17.

7. Lieutenant Colonel José María Mata, *Letter to Governor Juan Soto*, 30 July 1847, folder XI/481.3/1914, p. 156, Archivo de la Defensa Nacional, Mexico City, D.F.; Don Ramón Alcaraz, et al., *The Other Side: Or Notes for the History of the War between Mexico and the United States*, trans. Albert C. Ramsey (New York: John Wiley & Sons, 1850), 437–38.

8. Lieutenant Colonel José María Mata, letter to Governor Juan Soto, 25 July 1847, folder XI.481.3/2554, pp. 61–63, ADN.

9. Brooks, *Mexican War*, 454.

10. Ibid., 453–54.

11. Lieutenant Colonel Henry Wilson, letter to Brigadier General Roger Jones, 21 August 1847, American Military Operations in Mexico 1846–1848. Section G-220-X, 1, Justin H. Smith Collection, Diaries, Recollections, & Memoirs, Benson Latin American Collection, Austin, TX. BLAC.

12. Ibid., 2.

13. Randy W. Hackenburg, *Pennsylvania in the War with Mexico: The Volunteer Regiments* (Shippensburg, PA: White Mane Publishing Company, 1992), 67.

14. Major William Booth Taliaferro, Journal entry, 10 September 1847, The Aztec Club Archives Historical Papers, United States Army Military History Institute, Carlisle, Pa. Subsequently, Taliaferro rose to the rank of major general in the Confederate army.

15. Ibid.

16. Ibid.

17. Jacob J. Oswandel, *Notes of the Mexican War, 1846–47–48* (Philadelphia, 1885), 153.

18. Major General Winfield Scott, General Order No. 128, 30 April 1847, General Scott's Orders (41-1/2), War with Mexico 1847–1848, Entry Number 134, Records Group 94, Records of the Adjutant General's Office, National Archives and Records Administration, Washington, D.C. Here, Scott referred to the guerrillas as *rancheros* (ranchers) rather than the more pejorative term that would later come into widespread use, *banditti* (bandits).

19. Oswandel, *Notes*, 147–53.

20. Ethan Allen Hitchcock, *Diary*, 24 August 1847, Box 2, 50: 17–19, Gilcrease Museum of Western History, Tulsa, Okla.

21. Ibid. Hitchcock probably referred to Santo Domingo, Puebla.

22. Colonel Thomas Claiborne, "Colonel Thomas Claiborne's Memoirs Written When He was about Seventy Years of Age," Section G220-XV, 211, BLAC.

23. Commodore Matthew C. Perry, quoted by Samuel Eliot Morison in *"Old Bruin": Commodore Matthew Calbraith Perry, 1794–1858* (Boston: Little, Brown and Company, 1967), 238.

24. Colonel William Gates, Order 24, 27 March 1847, Mexican War—Orders 1845–1848, Volume 7, Tampico, March 1847–June 1848, Entry 134, Records Group 94, Records of the Adjutant General's Office, NARA I.

25. Colonel William Gates, Unnumbered order, 27 March 1847. Mexican War—Orders 1845–1848, Volume 7, Tampico, March 1847–June 1848, Entry 134, Records Group 94, Records of the Adjutant General's Office, NARA I.

26. General Gideon Pillow, General Order No. 38, Mexican War—Second Brigade, Volume 16, Second Division, 1846–1847, PI 17, Entry 134, Records Group 94, Records of the Adjutant Generals Office, NARA I.

27. The demoralizing effect of the guerrillas is attested to not only by officers such as the previously cited Major Taliaferro, but also by scholars of this period. The most recent work in this regard is Foos, *A Short, Offhand, Killing Affair.*

28. Castillo Lanras of the ministry of foreign relations, government, and police, letter to the minister of war and marine, 26 March 1846, folder 481.3/2868, p. 483, ADN.

29. *Mexiquense* refers to an inhabitant of the state of México. By contrast, a person identified solely as an inhabitant of the *nation* is a Mexicano.

30. Unsigned report, 26 July 1846, on gobierno del estado México letterhead to the President of the Republic, box 324, 1846, sin sección, AGN.

31. Illegibly signed report to the minister of interior relations and police, 22 July 1846, box 324, 1846, sin sección, AGN.

32. Illegibly signed letter to the minister of war and marine on comandancia general de México letterhead, 21 July 1846, folder 481.3/2868, p. 641, ADN.

33. Unsigned report of the operations section of the minister of war and marine, 30 March 1846, folder 481.3/2196, p. 468, ADN.

34. General Guzman, report to the minister of war and marine, 11 June 1846, folder 481.3/2229, p. 15, ADN.

35. General Francisco Pacheco, letter to the minister of war and marine, 14 July 1846, folder 481.3/2868, p. 259, ADN.

36. Ibid., 6 July 1846, folder 481.3/2868, p. 301, ADN.

37. José María Gonzales Mesa, letter to General Joaquín Rea and the minister of war and marine, 10 June 1846, folder 481.3/2868, p. 701, ADN.

38. General José de Ugarte, letter to the minister of war and marine, 17 July 1846, folder 481.3/2868, p. 526, ADN.

39. Ibid., 27 July 1846, folder 481.3/2868, pp. 538–39, ADN.

40. General Juan Álvarez, letter to the Ministry of War and Marine (no person cited), 24 August 1846, folder 481.3/2189, p. 00031, ADN.

41. Gobierno del estado de Chiapas [signature illegible], report to the minister of exterior relations, government, and police, box 3, 1847, sin sección, AGN.

42. José Ignacio Gueri[illegible] of the comandancia general del estado de Guanajuato, letter to the minister of war and marine, 22 January 1847, folder 481.3/2312, ADN.

43. Juan Diaz at the comandancia general de Oaxaca, letter to the minister of war and marine, 11 February 1847, folder 481.3/2349, p. 4, ADN.

44. Minister of exterior and interior relations, letter to the state of Puebla, 3 March 1847, file 19, box 337, 1847, sin sección, AGN.

45. Juan Álvarez, minister of exterior and interior relations, letter, 10 April 1847, folder 481.3/2493, p. 3, ADN.

46. Ibid., letter, 17 April 1847, folder 481.3/2493, p. 33, ADN.

47. Ibid., letter to the minister of war and marine, 3 May 1847, folder 481.3/2493, p. 35, ADN.

48. Ibid., letter to the substitute president of México, 10 May 1847, folder 481.3/2493, p. 42, ADN.

49. *Fodor's 1996 Guide to Mexico*, ed. Edie Jaolim (New York: Fodor's Publications, 1995), xlix.

50. William A. DePalo to author, *e-mail*, 29 April 1998.

51. Joaquin Angula of the Jaliscan state government, letter to the minister of exterior and interior relations, 10 February 1847, box 5, 1847, sin sección, AGN.

52. *La nueva era constitucional: Periodico del gobierno del estado libre de Oaxaca*, 24 February 1847, folder 6, box 339, 1847, sin sección, AGN.

53. Alcorta of the sección de operaciones del minsterio de guerra y marina, letter to the governor of Querétaro, 6 July 1847, documentos para la historia de México, Vol. 15, biblioteca, Hemeroteca Nacional de México, Mexico City. In an accusation best described as bizarre, the sección de operaciones accused Querétaro of failing to complete the enlistments because the queretarenses thought that the government planned to surrender to the U.S. Army. The official writing this letter did not address the obvious point that a government intent on surrender would not be requesting troops while it still had a large and functional national army.

54. Guillermo Landona of the comandancia general de Chiapas, report to the minister of war and marine, 30 July 1846, folder 481.3/2196, p. 403, ADN.

55. Governor Miguel Barbachano y Tarrazo, letter to the minister of war and marine, 16 December 1846, folder 481.3/2340, pp. 4–71, ADN.

56. Clyde G. Bushnell, "The Political and Military Career of Juan Álvarez, 1790–1867," (Ph.D. diss., University of Texas, 1958), 203. Álvarez subsequently defended his conduct on the grounds that a cavalry attack could have been "launched only when the enemy was breaking up" and that the American infantry formation was not broken because General Manuel Andrade had failed to launch a simultaneous attack as ordered by Álvarez himself. In turn, Andrade denied that Álvarez had the right to command him. However, later in the day, American cavalry maneuvered over the ground held earlier by Álvarez, thus proving that an attack could have been launched.

57. Ibid.

58. DePalo e-mail.

CHAPTER 4

The title of this chapter is taken from Luis de la Rosa's characterization of the state of public order in the territory of Tlaxcala during late 1847. Luis de la Rosa, letter to the minister of interior and exterior relations, 21 December 1847, box 334, folder 1, sin sección 1847, AGN. The epigraph appears in John Bartlett, *Bartlett's Familiar Quotations* (Boston: Little Brown, 1980), 826.

1. Friedrich Katz, *The Life and Times of Pancho Villa* (Palo Alto: Stanford University Press, 1998), 795–800. Katz concluded, "The Zapatista rebellion in Morelos basically consisted of peasants from free villages, largely excluding peons." He also demonstrated that the core of the Villista movement was composed of the free villagers and peons (peasants) of Chihuahua. Only after Pancho Villa's initial military successes did some members of the middle class join his ranks.

2. Carl von Clausewitz, *On War* (Princeton: Princeton University Press, 1976), 481–83.

3. Following the critical battle of September 13, 1847, in the Valley of México, the federal government left the capitol and set out for its temporary residence at Querétaro, some 125 miles to the north. The U.S. Army entered Mexico City the following day.

4. *Memoria de la hacienda de la republica Mexicana presentada a las cameras del ministro del ramo en julio de 1846, primera parte* (Mexico City: Imprenta de Ignacio Cumplido, 1846), inserted chart. The *alcabala* was a uniform head tax imposed on each Mexican. Given the polarized nature of México's socio-economic structure, this flat tax fell most heavily on the poor. During the course of the war, U.S. naval forces seized the Pacific ports of Guaymas, Mazatlán, and Acapulco as well as their Caribbean counterparts at Camargo, Tampico, Veracruz, and Tabasco.

5. Following the loss of the capitol, Santa Anna went to Orizaba to organize guerrillas. However, after decades as a general-of-the-line, he proved incapable of waging war with the flexibility and speed required in partisan warfare. Subsequently, he lost a set-piece battle at Huamantla to General Joseph Lane on October 8, 1847.

6. John Reese Kenly, *Memoirs of a Maryland Volunteer: War with Mexico in the Years 1846–1848* (Philadelphia: J. B. Lippincott & Company, 1873), 323.

7. Ethan Allen Hitchcock, *Diary*, 14 September 1847, Box 2, 50: 117–19, Gilcrease Museum of Western History, Tulsa, Okla.

8. Robert E. May, *John A. Quitman: Old South Crusader* (Baton Rouge: Louisiana State University Press, 1985), 195.

9. Justin H. Smith, *The War with Mexico*, rev. ed. (1919; repr., Gloucester, Mass.: Peter Smith, 1963), 2: 167. José Maria Tornel y Medevil (1789–1853) served México as a diplomat, minister of war, general, politician and educator during a long and varied career. He issued his order to release the prisoners in his capacity as a member of the federal cabinet. *Diccionario porrúa de historia, biografia y geografiá de México* (Mexico City: Editorial Porrúa, 1995), 4: 3542.

10. George Ballantine, *The Mexican War by an English Soldier Comprising Incidents and Adventures in the United States and Mexico with the American Army* (New York: W. A. Townsend, 1860), 272.

11. Winfield Scott, *Executive Document 56 of the House of Representatives— Messages from the President of the United States Transmitting Reports from the Secretary of State and the Secretary of War With Accompanying Documents in Compliance With the Resolution of the 7th February, 1848* (Washington: Wendell and Van Benthuysen, March 20, 1848), 219.

12. José María Roa Barcena, *Recuerdos de la invasión norteamericana: 1846–1848* (Mexico City: Editorial Porrúa, 1971), 3: 168.

13. Ibid.

14. General Joseph Lane, *Report of 22 October 1847, Executive Document Number 1, Report of the Secretary of War to the Thirtieth Congress* (Washington, D.C.: Wendell and Van Benthuysen), 481. Unlike counterparts such as General David Emanuel Twiggs, Lane understood that only equally mobile pursuers could defeat the rapidly moving partisan formations. His reliance upon cavalry and Mexican auxiliaries foreshadowed some aspects of modern counter-guerrilla warfare. Joaquín Rea's substantial military experience included service in both the War of Independence as a protégé of General Nicolas Bravo and subsequent campaigning against Juan Álvarez in 1842. Throughout his career, he remained a steadfast conservative and a supporter of his mentor.

15. Lieutenant Colonel George W. Hughes, Untitled report, 13 September 1847, Adjutant General's Files, 118, American Military Operations in Mexico, 1846–1848, G220-IX, Benson Latin American Collection, University of Texas, Austin.

16. Lieutenant Colonel George W. Hughes, Untitled report, 13 September 1847, Adjutant General's Files, 117, American Military Operations in Mexico, 1846–1848, G220-IX, BLAC.

17. Smith, *War with Mexico*, 2: 156.

18. Secretary of War William Learned Marcy to General Winfield Scott, Order, 6 October 1847, in Kenly, *Memoirs of a Maryland Volunteer*, 309.

19. Lieutenant Colonel Dixon H. Miles, letter, 5 January, 1848, Executive Document Number 56, 259; British Ambassador Percy Doyle, letter to General William O. Butler, Letters Received from Officers 1847–1848—Mexican War, Entry Group 134, Records Group 94, NARA I. In George Towne Baker, III, "Mexico City and the War with the United States: A Study in the Politics of Military Occupation," Ph.D. diss., Duke University, 1970, 286.

20. Executive Document 56, 259 (Washington, D.C.: Library of Congress).

21. General David E. Twiggs, letter to General Roger Jones, 5 January 1848, Document number T-37, Letters Received by the Adjutant General's Office, microcopy M-567, roll 393, National Archives and Records Administration, College Park, Md.

22. General William Orlando Butler, letters to Ambassador Percy Doyle, 13 April 1848, and 16 April 1848, Butler Letters of February–July 1848, Mexican War, 1845–1850, Entry Number 134, Records Group 94, NARA I.

23. Jacob J. Oswandel, *Notes of the Mexican War 1846–1847–1848* (Philadelphia, 1885), 216.

24. John James Peck, *The Sign of the Eagle: A View of Mexico, 1830–1855* (San Diego: Union-Tribune, 1970), 152. Subsequently, Peck rose to the rank of major general in the Union Army.

25. Randy W. Hackenburg, *Pennsylvania in the War with Mexico: The Volunteer Regiments* (Shippensburg, PA: White Mane Publishing Company, 1992), 79.

26. Zachary Taylor, *Letters of Zachary Taylor from the Battlefields of the Mexican War* (1908; Reprint, New York: Krauss Reprint Company, 1970), 148. In the preceding description, Taylor referred to the attackers as "bandits." That characterization remains inaccurate. Bandits seek material gain, preferably with minimal risk. By contrast, the Mexicans cited in this particular dispatch attacked soldiers with no assets other than horses and the arms they were carrying. The attackers were guerrillas, not bandits. For the field report of this encounter, see Lieutenant R. P. Campbell to Major (illegible), Report, 3 November 1847, Frame T-601 microcopy number 567, roll 363, NARA I.

27. John Frost, *The History of Mexico and Its Wars* (New Orleans: Armand Hawkins, 1882), 622–24.

28. Ibid., 625.

29. Ibid., 616. "About the middle of December, a body of Americans were attacked near Mazatlán [Sinaloa–Author's note] by some guerrilla, led by an officer named Mejares. He was killed and his men repulsed with considerable loss."

30. U.S. Pacific Squadron Commander William Branford Shubrick, letter citing the report of Colonel Henry Burton, 18 December 1847 , Executive Document Number 56, 273 (Washington, D.C.: Library of Congress).

31. Ibid., 273–74. "By the last of May the ships must leave this harbor; as the squadron is at present, it cannot spare men enough to leave a sufficient garrison; if not reinforced; we much evacuate and thus lose the most important port on the Pacific."

32. Don Ramón Alcaraz, ed., *The Other Side: Or Notes for the History of the War between Mexico and the United States,* trans. Albert C. Ramsey (New York: John Wiley, 1850), 442.

33. The quartermaster of the Army subsequently asked that Congress provide survivor's pensions to the families of U.S. civilians killed on convoy duty in Mexico. *Executive Documents Printed by Order of the Senate of the United States during the First Session of the Thirtieth Congress Begun and Held at the City of Washington, December 6, 1846 in Eight Volumes,* (Washington, D.C.: Wendell and Van Benthuysen, 1847), 549.

34. Ibid., 442.

35. Frost, *History of Mexico and Its Wars,* 626.

36. Scott, letter to Taylor, 24 April 1847, Executive Document Number 56, 139.

37. General Winfield Scott, General Order No. 372, 12 December 1847, Orders and Special Orders–Headquarters of the Army–War with Mexico 1847–1848, Entry Number 134, Records Group 94, Records of the Adjutant General's Office, NARA I.

38. General John E. Wool, Circular, 25 July 1847, Adjutant General's Files, 124, American Military Operations in Mexico, 1846–1848, G220-IX, BLAC.

39. Ephraim Kirby Smith, *To Mexico with Scott: Letters of Captain E. Kirby Smith to His Wife* (Cambridge: Harvard University Press, 1917), 51.

40. General John E. Wool, Order Number 11, 17 December 1847, W-1025, microcopy M, roll 367, Letters Received by the Adjutant General's Office, NARA I.

41. General John E. Wool, Untitled report, 20 December 1847, Adjutant General's Files, 125, American Military Operations in Mexico, 1846–1848, G220-IX, BLAC.

42. William Learned Marcy, letter, 9 July 1846, Thirtieth Congress, First Session Executive Document No. 60, *Messages of the President of the United States* (Washington, D.C.: Wendell and Van Benthuysen, 1848), 157. However, Marcy also clearly indicated that such efforts as his commanders might make in conciliating the Mexicans in no way ought to interfere with the military business at hand. In the same letter, he stated, "The management of these delicate matters is confided to your discretion, but they are not to paralyze the military arm, or in any degree to arrest or retard your military movements. These must proceed vigorously."

43. For a general discussion of this subject, see Carlos Rodriguez Vinegas, "Las fianzas publicas," in *México al tiempo de su guerra con los estados unidos (1846–1848),* ed. Joséfina Zoraida Vásquez (Mexico City: El Colegio de México,

Secretaría de Relaciones Exteriores, Fondo de Cultura Económica Fundación, 1998), 124. The implementation of this decree might well have proved as disastrous as a similar effort in 1804. However, the damage done by merely promulgating such a directive served as a catalyst for reopening sharp divisions among Mexicans. Scott took appropriate advantage of the situation.

44. Ibid., 124–25.

45. Proclamation, Office of the Civil and Military Governor, *El monitor republicano*, 23 November 1847, Hemeroteca Nacional de México, Mexico City. The order read: "The army of the United States having become possessed of the city of Mexico and its neighborhood, on the 14th of September last, all the rights and authority of the Mexican Government in and over the district so occupied; vested in the United States; consequently no sale of ecclesiastical property, described in the above decree is valid unless made with the consent of the authorities of the United States, and in the form and under the conditions expressed."

46. Scott, General Order 297, 24 September 1847, American Military Operations in México, 41.5: 26, Section G220-IX, BLAC.

47. Letters exchanged between General Winfield Scott and Juan Manuel, archbishop of Caesarea, Executive Document 56, 244–49.

48. Moses Y. Beach, editor of the *New York Sun*, was an enthusiastic supporter of the Polk administration.

49. Moses Y. Beach, letter to James Buchanan, 14 June 1847, Records Group 59, Records of the Department of State–Dispatches from Special Agents of the Department of State, 1794–1906, Volumes 14–15, Microfilm M37-7, NARA II.

50. Hitchcock, *Diary*, 14 September 1847, Box 2, 50: 117-119, GMWH.

51. Major General J. A. Quitman, Proclamation, 22 September 1847, box 1, folder 2 1847, sin clasificación, AGN.

52. Quitman, Proclamation, 6 October 1847, box 211, dossier 135, AGN.

53. Antonio López de Santa Anna, "La atalaya de Xalapa," p. 4, column 3, in "Political, Social, Economic, and Military Conditions in Mexico, 1844–1848," 504, G220-XIX, BLAC. *Hombres de bien* is an idiomatic term that refers to Mexicans with the education, manners, occupation, and income to participate in the political, economic, and social life at the top of México's socio-economic pyramid.

54. B. J. Y. M. Bocanegra, "Diario de la entrada de los Americanos a la capital," in "Political, Social, and Economic Conditions in Mexico, 1844–1848," G220-XVII, BLAC.

55. Baker, "Mexico City and the War with the United States," 179.

56. Hitchcock, *Diary*, 28 January 1848, Box 2, 51: 5–7, GMWH.

57. Actos del cabildo, volumen 59, Archivo Histórico del Municipio Xalapa, Xalapa, Veracruz, México.

58. Actos del cabildo, volumen 59: 154, AHMX, Xalapa.

59. Actos del cabildo, volumen 59: 104, AHMX, Xalapa.

60. General Francisco de Garay of the Linea Militar de Huejutla, letter, 14 November 1847, folder 481.3/2772, p. 148, ADN.

61. de Garay, letter, 4 December 1847, folder XI/481.3/2772, p. 00154, ADN.

62. Jean Meyer, cited by Daniel Molino Álvarez, *La passion del padre Jarauta* (Mexico City: Gobierno de la Ciudad de Mexico, 1999), 108–109.

63. Ibid.

64. Ibid.

65. Minister of Interior and Exterior Relations Manuel de la Peña y Peña, letter to Don Jesus Cardenas, commissioner of the state of Tamaulipas, 16 November 1847, folder XI.481.3/2739, p. 20, ADN.

66. José de Aranda of the Deputation of Zacatecas, letter to the minister of interior and exterior relations, 1 December 1847, box 334, file E3 1847, sin sección, AGN.

67. Joaquin Zarco of La Comandancia Militar de las Fuerzas del Estado, letter to the minister of war and marine, 27 January 1848, folder XI.481.3/2776, pp. 5–6, ADN.

68. J. Naf. Guerra of the gobierno del estado libre y soberano de Puebla, report to the minister of war and marine, 21 January 1848, folder XI/481.3/2772, pp. 6 and 23, ADN.

69. Jean Meyer, cited by Alvarez, *La passion del padre Jarauta*, 108–109.

70. Ibid.

71. Leticia Reina, *Las rebeliones campesinas on México, 1819–1906* (Mexicio City: Siglo Veintiuno, 1980), 363–65.

72. Mario Vanalioa, letter to Minister of War and Marine Pedro Maria Anaya, 26 May 1848, folder XI/481/3/2809, pp. 1–2, ADN.

73. Transcript, 4 September 1847, in Letters Received by Colonel Childs, Civil and Military Governor of Puebla 1847–1848—Army of Occupation—Mexican War— Office of the Adjutant General, Box 12, Entry 133, Records Group 94, pp. 1–2, NARA I.

74. Ibid., 1.

75. Ibid., 2–3.

76. Actos secretos, 4 January 1848, Archivo Histórico Municipal de Toluca de Lerdo, Toluca, México state.

77. Actos del cabildo (1847), 59: 104, AHMX, Xalapa.

78. Tomas Marin of the Comandancia General del Estado de Veracruz, letter to the minister of war and marine, 15 November 1847, folder XI/481.3/2715, p. 20, ADN.

79. Mariano Senobio, letter, 22 November 1847, folder XI/481.3/1914, p. 520, ADN.

80. Actos del cabildo (1847), 59: 154, AHMX.

81. Guillermo Morales at Linares, letter to the minister of relations, 31 December 1847, folder E10, box 350, 1848, sin sección, AGN.

82. Mora in Querétaro, letter, 29 October 1847, folder XI/481.3/1914, pp. 459–60, ADN.

83. Governor Lorenzo Arellano of Guanajuato, Proclamation, 3 December 1847, Box 326, 1847, sin sección, AGN.

84. Ibid.

85. Eric Hobsbawm devoted considerable attention to the real and assumed relation-ship between such robbery and political violence, particularly in his book *Banditry* (New York: Delacorte Press, 1969). A study of any linkages between these two practices in the Guanajuato of 1847 awaits a review of relevant material in that state's archives.

86. Minister of the Hacienda Luis de la Rosa, letter to the minister of interior and exterior relations, 21 December 1847, box 334, 1847, sin sección, AGN.

87. Ibid.

88. Juan Álvarez, letter, 2 February 1848, folder XI/481.3/2776, p. 17, ADN.

CHAPTER 5

The epigraph comes from James K. Polk, *Message from the President of the United States to the Two Houses of Congress at the Commencement of the Thirtieth Congress, December 7, 1847* (Washington, D.C.: Van Benthuysen, 1847), 16.

1. See chapter three for a detailed review of this proclamation.
2. Lieutenant Walter L. Biscoe, letter, 1 March 1848, Letters Received by the Adjutant General's Office 1822–1860, year 1848, document 119T (old index) microcopy number M-567, roll 394, NARA I.
3. *The American Star*, 9 February 1848, citing a Mexican newspaper published in Chihuahua, Chihuahua, El Faro, Hemeroteca Nacional de México, Mexico City.
4. *The American Star*, 19 April 1848, HNM.
5. *The American Star*, 20 April 1848, HNM.
6. General Joaquín Rea to the minister of war and marine, letter, 10 February 1848, folder XI/481.3/2744, pp. 5–6, ADN.
7. Cristobal Andrade, prefect of the district of Huehuetla, to the minister of war and marine, letter, 2 March 1848, Document H/252(73:72)/184, Archivo General de la Secretaría de Relaciones Exteriores, Manuscripts Section, Library of Congress, Washington, D.C.
8. General William Orlando Butler, General Order Number 3, in *The American Star*, 22 February 1848, HNM.
9. General William Orlando Butler, letters, February–July 1848, Letters Sent, Mexican War, 1845–1848, volume 2, PI-17, Entry Group 130, Records Group 94, NARA I.
10. *Memoria del secretario de estado y del despacho de guerra y marina leide en la camera de diputados el día 9 y en la de senadores el 11 de enero de 1849* (Mexico City: Imprenta de Vicente Garcia Torres en el Ex-Convento del Espíritu Santo, 1849), pp. 8–9, Biblioteca Nacional, AGN.
11. Justin H. Smith, *The War with México*, rev. ed. (1919; repr., Gloucester, Mass.: Peter Smith, 1963). 2: 142.
12. Governor Miguel Barbachano to the minister of war and marine, letter, 24 June 1848, folder 2820, section XI/ 481.3, pp. 4–6, ADN.
13. Governor Miguel Barbachano to the minister of war and marine, letter, 17 April 1848, folder 5, box 356, 1846, sin sección, AGN.
14. Nelson A. Reed, *The Caste War of Yucatán* (Palo Alto, Calif.: Stanford University Press, 2001), 12.
15. Ibid., 31–37.
16. Justo Sierra O'Reilly to James Buchanan, letter, 7 March 1848, cited by William R. Manning, ed., *Diplomatic Correspondence of the United States: Inter-American Affairs, 1831–1860*, volume 8, document 3755, México (Washington, D.C.: Carnegie Endowment for International Peace, 1937), 1071.
17. Santiago Mendez to James Buchanan, letter, 25 March 1848, cited by Manning, *Diplomatic Correspondence*, volume 8, document 3756, México, 1073–74.
18. Ibid.
19. *The American Star*, 11 April 1848, HNM.
20. Ibid., 433. In 1846, Yucatán had declared its neutrality in the war between México and the United States. *Diccionario porrúa de historia, biografia y geografiá de México* (Mexico City: Editorial Porrúa, 1995), 4: 3277–78.

21. Governor Miguel Barbachano to the minister of war and marine, letter, 14 June 1848, folder XI/481.3/2820, pp. 4–6, ADN.

22. Secretary of State James Buchanan to Nathan Clifford, U.S. minister to México, dispatch, 7 August 1848, cited by Manning, *Diplomatic Correspondence*, volume 9, document 3772, México, 4.

23. Ibid. The Huasteca consists of parts of five states: southern Tamaulipas, northern Veracruz, eastern San Luis Potosí, and small parts of Hidalgo and Querétaro. This is the area in which the coastal plain joins the slopes of the Sierra Madre Oriental.

24. Minister of the Interior and Exterior Luis de la Rosa to the minister of war and marine, letter, 9 May 1848, folder 2772, section XI/481.3, pp. 46–48, ADN.

25. Ibid.

26. Ibid.

27. The Sierra Gorda is a mountainous region encompassing part of western Guanajuato, eastern Querétaro, and southern San Luis Potosí.

28. General Francisco de Garay, the Linea Militaria de Huehuetla, to the minister of war and marine, letter, 31 November 1847, folder XI/481.3/2772, p. 148, ADN.

29. Juan Amades to the minister of war and marine, letter, folder 2807, section XI/481.3, pp. 68–72, ADN.

30. Comandancia general de Querétaro to the minister of war and marine, letter, 27 October 1848, folder 2890, section XI/481.3, p. 51, ADN.

31. Captain Anastasio Llorente, letter, 3 July 1848, folder 2, box 357, 1848, sin sección, AGN.

32. Sebastian Zarinas, government of the state of Puebla, letter summarizing Llorente's report, 28 May 1848, folder 2, box 357, 1848, sin sección, AGN.

33. Ibid.

34. *The American Star*, 7 March 1848, HNM.

35. Ibid.

36. Major Folliott T. Lally at Tampico to Major Lorenzo Thomas, letter, 8 April 1848, Letters Received from Officers A–K, Mexican War, Army of Occupation, Entry Group 133, Records Group 94, Office of the Adjutant General, NARA I.

37. Ibid.

38. Colonel Newman S. Clarke, dispatch, 6 March 1848, Department of Cuernavaca, Letters Sent 1845–1848, Mexican War 1845–1850, volume 6, Entry Group 130, Records of the Adjutant General's Office 1790–1917, NARA I.

39. Ibid. Italics added.

40. Ibid.

41. Ibid.

42. Captain Samuel P. Heintzelman, *S. P. Heintzelman Journal 1847–1850*, LCMSS, Washington, D.C. Heintzelman subsequently rose to the rank of major general in the Union Army.

43. Juan R. Llorente, commander of the district police force, to the Mexican army's Sección de Operaciones, report, 20 June 1848, folder XI/481.3/2482, p. 48, ADN.

44. *The American Star*, 7 March 1848, HNM.

45. Eric J. Hobsbawm, *Social Bandits and Primitive Rebels: Studies of Archaic Forms of Social Movements in the 19th and 20th Centuries* (Glencoe, Ill.: The Free Press, 1959), 5.

46. Samuel Chamberlain, *My Confession: Recollections of a Rogue*, ed. William H. Goetzmann (Austin: Texas State Historical Association, 1996), 264–69.

47. Captain Kenton Harper, report, 28 March 1848, *Letters Received from Officers L–Z*, Mexican War, Army of Occupation, Entry Group 133, Records of the Adjutant General's Office 1790–1917, NARA I. Harper probably meant Paras, Nuevo León.

48. *The American Star*, 18 April 1848, HNM.

49. Colonel Bankhead, Order Number 100 issued in Orizaba, Veracruz, 17 May 1848, G220-Volume IX, BLAC.

50. Major General John Ellis Wool, Special Order 196, 3 April 1848, General Wool's Orders and Special Orders, Mexican War, Army of Occupation, Entry Group 44, Record Group 94, Office of the Adjutant General, NARA I.

51. Receipt signed by Juan Mugioa, 7 June 1848, sheet 7, folder 13, box 349, 1848 (stored in an "1846" box), sin sección, AGN.

52. General Persifor F. Smith, Special Order 39, Orders, 1845–1848, Vera Cruz, May–August 1848, volume 10, Mexican War 1845–1850, Records of the Adjutant General's Office 1780–1917, Records Group 94, NARA I.

53. Ibid.

54. Richard Griswold del Castillo, *The Treaty of Guadalupe Hidalgo: A Legacy of Conflict* (Norman: University of Oklahoma Press, 1990), 187.

55. Manuel Hernandez, government of Puebla state to the minister of war and marine, letter, 8 July 1848, folder XI/481.3/2825, p. 2, ADN.

56. Robert E. Lee to John Mackay, letter, 2 October 1847, Robert E. Lee Papers, United States Army Military History Institute, Carlisle, Penn.

57. Major General John Ellis Wool, Order 94, 27 March 1848, General Wool's Orders and Special Orders, Mexican War, Army of Occupation, Entry Group 44, Record Group 94, Office of the Adjutant General, NARA I.

58. Cristobal Andrade to the minister of interior and exterior relations, letter, 2 June 1848, file 1, box 349, 1848, sin sección, AGN.

59. Polk, *Message . . . December 7, 1847*, 13.

60. Winfield Scott, *Memoirs of Lieut.-General Scott, LL.D.* (New York: Sheldon & Company Publishers, 1864), 2: 560.

61. John Reese Kenly, *Memoirs of a Maryland Volunteer: War with México in the Years 1846–1848* (Philadelphia: J.B. Lippincott & Company, 1873), 264.

62. Price subsequently served as governor of Missouri and as a major general in the Confederate Army.

63. José Mariá Roa Barcena, *Recuerdos de la invasion noreteamericana: 1846–1848* (Mexico City: Editorial Porrúa, 1971), 2: 187–90.

64. Cadmus M. Wilcox, *History of the Mexican War* (Washington, D.C.: Church News, 1892), 538–44.

65. Following an exchange of heated communications between the commands of the two national armies, Price returned to his position of February 2, 1848.

66. This information is found in Table 2.1.

67. The calculations are as follows:

Population of Chihuahua (147,600) divided by that of México (7,016,300)
147,600 / 7,016,300 = 2.1037%
2.1037% divided into 100 = 47.53529
47.53529 multiplied by 700 (volunteers) = 33,274 men

68. Samuel Elliot Morison, *"Old Bruin" Commodore Matthew Calbraith Perry, 1794–1858* (Boston: Little, Brown & Company, 1967), 201.

69. Albert G. Brackett, *General Lane's Brigade in México* (Cincinnati: H. W. Derby & Co. and New York: J. C. Derby, 1854), 292.

70. The importance of Calhoun's opposition is fully examined by John Douglas Pitts Fuller in *The Movement for the Acquisition of All México 1846–1848* (Baltimore: Johns Hopkins Press, 1936).

71. John Douglas Pitts Fuller, "The Slavery Question and the Movement to Acquire México, *Mississippi Valley Historical Review* 21, June 1934: 46.

72. *The American Star*, 24 December 1847, HNM.

73. Reginald Horsman, *Race and Manifest Destiny: The Origins of American Racial Anglo-Saxonism* (Cambridge: Harvard University Press, 1981), 242.

74. James K. Polk and others, Executive Document Number 59 of the House of Representatives, Correspondence between the Secretary of War and General Scott. Message of the President of the United States transmitting the correspondence between the Secretary of War and Major General Scott, with the accompanying documents in compliance with the resolution of the House of Representatives on the 17th instant, April 26, 1848, 9.

75. Ibid.

76. Polk, *Diary*, ed. Quaife, 3: 347–48. Polk refers to House of Representatives vote of January 3, 1848, passed by an 85–81 margin, charging him with having "unjustly and unconstitutionally" begun the war, an accusation he believed to be false.

77. Albert Gallatin, *Expenses of the War* (Washington, D.C.: J. Tower Printers, 1848), 13–14.

78. Mariano Venalioa to the minister of war and marine, letter, 26 May 1848, folder XI/481.3/2809, pp. 1–2, ADN.

79. *Diccionario porrúa*, 3: 2637–38.

80. Comandancia General del Sur Juan Álvarez, letter, 11 August 1848, folder XI/481.3/2873, p. 294, ADN.

81. A year earlier, Bustamante's planned expedition to California ended prematurely when he received orders to respond to the 1847 rebellion in Mazatlán, Sinaloa. *Diccionario porrúa*, 1: 500.

82. *Memoria del secretario del estado y del despacho de guerra y marina leide en la camera de diputados el día 9 y en la de senadores el 11 de enero de 1849*, 6.

83. Ibid.

84. Sheet 3, folder 1, series 1849, AHEM, Toluca, México.

CHAPTER 6

The epigraph comes from Sherman Edwards and Peter Stone, *1776: A Musical Play* (New York: Viking Press, 1970).

1. This immigrant artist signed his works as Carl Nebel in the United States and as Carlos Nebel in México.

2. *Memoria del secretario del estado y del despacho de guerra y marina leide en la camera de diputados el día 9 y en la de senadores el 11 de enero de 1849* (Mexico City: Imprenta de Vicente Garcia Torres en el Ex-Convento del Espíritu Santo, 1846), 6–9. Biblioteca Nacional, Archivo General de la Nación, Mexico City.

3. Moses Y. Beach, Letter to Secretary of State James Buchanan, 4 June 1847, Volumes 14–15, M37-7, Dispatches from Special Agents of the Department of State 1794–1906, Records of the Department of State, Records Group 59, NARA II.

4. James K. Polk, *The Diary of James K. Polk during His Presidency, 1845 to 1849*, ed. Milo Milton Quaife (Chicago: A.C. McClurg& Company, 1910), 3: 216.

5. Manuel Crescencio Rejon, "Observation of the Treaty of Guadalupe Hidalgo," in *The View from Chapultepec–Mexican Writers on the Mexican-American War*, ed. Cecil Robinson (Tucson: The University of Arizona Press, 1989), 96.

6. Ibid., 97–100.

7. Charles Allen Smart, *Viva Juárez: A Biography* (Philadelphia: Lippincott, 1963), 276.

8. Ethan Allen Hitchcock, *Diary*, February-March 1848, Box 2, 51: 23, Gilcrease Museum of Western History, Tulsa, Okla.

9. John H. Coatsworth, "Measuring Influence," in *Rural Revolt in México: U.S. Intervention and the Domain of Subaltern Politics*, ed. Daniel Nugent (Durham: Duke University Press, 1988), 68.

APPENDIX A

1. Mansfield's books about the conflict include *The Mexican War—A History of Its Origins* (New York: A. S. Barnes & Co., 1850) and *Life and Services of General Winfield Scott, Including the Siege of Veracruz, the Battle of Cerro Gordo, and the Battles in the Valley of México, to the Conclusion of Peace and His Return to the United States* (New York: S. Barnes & Co., 1850).

BIBLIOGRAPHIC ESSAY

1. Francis Baylies, *A Narrative of Major General Wool's Campaign in Mexico in the Years 1846, 1847, and 1848* (Albany, N.Y.: Little & Company, 1851, repr., Austin, Tex.: Jenkins, Publishing Company, 1975); Jacob S. Robinson, *A Journal of the Santa Fe Expedition under Colonel Doniphan* (1932; New York: Da Capo Press, 1972).

2. James Schoular, *History of the United States under the Constitution* (1880; repr., New York: Kraus Reprint Company, 1970).

3. Horatio O. Ladd, *History of the War with México* (New York: Dodd, Mead & Company, 1882), 322.

4. Justin H. Smith, *The War with México*, rev. ed. (1919; repr., Gloucester, Mass.: Peter Smith, 1963).

5. For example, he substantiated his assertions that México sought war with the United States by citing bellicose statements from politicians and generals who were not in the highest councils of Mexico's government when the war began. Also, he did not refer to publicly available documents in which some of those officials expressed their anxiety about the outcome of such a conflict.

6. Richard Griswold del Castillo, *The Treaty of Guadalupe Hidalgo: A Legacy of Conflict* (Norman: University of Oklahoma Press, 1990).

7. Albert K. Weinberg, *Manifest Destiny: A Study of Nationalist Expansion in American History* (Baltimore: The Johns Hopkins University Press, 1935).

8. Ward McAfee and J. Cordell Robinson, *Origins of the Mexican War: A Documentary Source Book* (Salisbury, N.C.: Documentary Publications, 1982).

9. Pedro Santoni, *Mexicans at Arms: Puro Federalists and the Politics of War, 1845–1848* (Fort Worth: Texas Christian University Press, 1996).

10. Mañuel Balbontín, *La invasión americana: apuntes de subteniente de artillería Mañuel Balbontín* (Mexico City: Tipografía de Gonzalo A. Esteva, 1888).

11. Carlos María de Bustamante, *El nuevo Bernal Diaz del Castillo, o sea, la historia de la invasion de los angloamericanos en México* (1847; reprint, Mexico City: Consejo nacional para la cultura y las artes, 1997).

12. "El sistema de guerrilla como defense," letter to the minister of interior and exterior relations, 30 April 1847, in *Obras completas de don Melchor Ocampo: documentos politicos y familiares, 1842–1851*, ed. Raul Arreola Cortes (Morelia, México: Comite Editorial del Gobierno de Michoacán, 1986), 3: 189–90. Numerous war-related materials are found in *Obras completas*.

13. José Fernando Ramirez, *Mexico durante su guerra con los Estados Unidos* (Mexico City: Vda de C. Bouret, 1905), and *México during the War with the United States*, ed. Walter V. Scholes, trans. Elliot B. Scherr (Columbia: University of Missouri Press, 1950).

14. Ramón Alcaraz, ed., *Apuntes para la historía de la guerra entre México y los Estados Unidos* (1848; repr., Mexico City: Siglo Vientiuno Editores, 1970).

15. Ramón Alcaraz, ed., *The Other Side: Or Notes for the History of the War between Mexico and the United States*, trans. Albert C. Ramsey (New York: John Wiley, 1850).

16. José María Roa Barcena, *Recuerdos de la invasion norteamericana, 1846–1848*, (Mexico City: Editorial Porrúa, 1971).

17. Thomas R. Hietala, *Manifest Destiny: Anxious Aggrandizement in Late Jacksonian America* (Ithaca, N.Y.: Cornell University Press, 1995); Myra Jehlen, *American Incarnation: The Individual, the Nation, and the Continent* (Cambridge, Mass.: Harvard University Press, 1986); Walter A. McDougall, *Promised Land, Crusader State: The American Encounter with the World Since 1776* (Boston: Houghton Mifflin Company, 1997); Anders Stephanson, *Manifest Destiny: American Expansionism and the Empire of Right* (New York: Hill and Wang, 1995); R. W. Van Alstyne, *The Rising American Empire* (New York: Oxford University Press, 1960); Weinberg, *Manifest Destiny*; William Appleman Williams, *From Colony to Empire: Essays in the History of American Foreign Relations* (New York: John Wiley & Sons, Inc., 1937).

18. Gaston Garcia Cantu, *Las invasiones norteamericanos en México* (Mexico City: Fonda de Cultura Económica y Secretaría de la Defensa Naciónal, 1996).

19. Alcaraz, *Other Side*, 2.

20. Roa Barcena, *Recuerdos*, 3: 341.

21. *Diccionario porrúa*, 4: 2972–73.

22. Roa Barcena, *Recuerdos*, 3: 340–41.

23. Joséfina Zoraida Vásquez, ed., *México al tiempo de su guerra con los estados unidos (1846–1848)* (Mexico City: Secretaría de Relaciones Exteriores–Fondo de Cultura Económica, 1997), 45–46.

24. Ibid., 46.

25. Laura Herrera Serna, ed., *México en guerra 1846–1848: Perspectivas regionales* (Mexico City: Museo Naciónal de las intervenciones and Consejo nacional para la cultura y las artes, 1997).

26. Maria Gayon Cordova, *La occupación yanqui de la ciudad de Mexico, 1847–1848*, (Mexico City: Instituto nacional de antropología e história and Consejo nacional para la cultura y las artes, 1997).

27. In *Las rebeliones*, Reina discusses such rebellions during the 1819–1906 period.

For more than 150 years, historians of this war on both sides of the Rio Grande often have reached conclusions as stark and simple as those of Carlos Nebel's painting. The first U.S. histories of the war reflected a triumphant and expansionist sentiment. That particular perspective mirrored popular opinion of the time. Writers of the era—Nathan Covington Brooks, John L. Frost, John S. Jenkins, Edward Mansfield, and Brantz Meyer—produced celebratory works that placed far greater emphasis on nationalist pride than on scholarly objectivity. A considerable portion of the published literature of the period focused upon the military aspects of the war, with the works of Francis Baylies and Jacob S. Robinson being typical of this genre.[1]

Officers and enlisted men who served in the war supplemented literary efforts of their civilian counterparts. Major Robert Anderson, Samuel Chamberlain, Colonel Samuel Ryan Curtis, Lieutenant Henry W. Halleck, Ralph W. Kirkham, Jacob Oswandel, and Captain Ephraim Kirby Smith all produced well-written memoirs. Veterans frequently provided more pointed and balanced histories than did contemporary scholars. For example, Anderson wrote in explicit detail of the carnage inflicted upon the civilians of Veracruz by Scott's siege artillery. Unlike some authors, he did not gloss over the effects of the bombardment by merely noting the speed with which the U.S. Army forced the surrender of the city and its garrison.

Invariably, American historians of the conflict reflected the temper of their times. Frequently, late-nineteenth-century scholars treated the 1846–48 war in the framework of the pervasive disputes about the Civil

War. For example, a preeminent northern historian such as James Schoular interpreted the war with México as a southern effort to expand the territory in which slavery could be practiced.[2] By contrast, southern partisans such as Alfred Jeremiah Beveridge, a noted author and U.S. senator, insisted that considerations of slavery were factors of no consequence in the origins or course of the conflict. This dispute lasted well into the twentieth century. In 1934, John D. P. Fuller continued Beveridge's defense of the South. In 1980, Ernest McPherson Lander took these arguments one step further, contending that the South Carolinians of that era were mightily concerned about the negative effects of the war on slavery. He argued that their publicly voiced doubts constrained Polk's territorial ambitions.

However, even the fierce disputations between historians such as Beveridge and Schoular failed to overshadow the generally triumphant tone with which late-nineteenth-century historians addressed the war. Typical of those writers is Horatio O. Ladd. Even though he conceded that the United States provoked a violent Mexican response by sending troops in the Nueces Strip, he wrote: "On the other hand, the grandeur of a Christian republic that in a hundred years may hold three hundred millions in its borders, stretching from the Atlantic to the Pacific shores over such a magnificent domain, will ever, over the graves of the heroes of the Mexican War, inspire patriot hearts to the severest toils and the largest sacrifices for their country."[3]

The 1919 publication of Justin H. Smith's *The War with Mexico* marked the apogee of this perspective.[4] In this work, the author concluded that México's actions left the United States no honorable alternative other than war. He deemed the subsequent confiscation of approximately half of that nation's territory to be just compensation for the unpaid claims of his aggrieved fellow citizens. Most controversially, he described Mexicans using stereotypical and racist imagery. For decades, Smith's work enjoyed such widespread acceptance that the veracity of his research remained unquestioned for some time.[5] Other early-twentieth-century historians shared some of Smith's biases. For example, in 1913 George Lockhart Rives wrote an elegantly phrased and well-researched history of the conflict in which he concluded that Mexicans bore responsibility for the war because they refused to yield peaceably and promptly to the inevitable triumph of the United States. This argument rests upon the implicit assumption that México did not possess the most basic prerogative of a sovereign nation: to maintain the integrity of its national territory.

A countervailing historiography of the war gradually developed during the middle and latter part of the twentieth century. This development can be attributed in some degree to the social and political changes that transformed the national political landscape during the 1960s and 1970s. These included not only the destruction of legalized segregation at the hands of the Civil Rights Movement but also changes in individual social behavior—symbolized by the widespread rejection of traditional gender roles and the willingness to challenge U.S. policy in Vietnam. Concurrently, many academicians began rejecting the instinctive glorification of the nation's past that characterized the traditional cold war mentality. In this changed milieu, scholars questioned the prevailing interpretations of the past. Here, many historians merit mention.

In *The Treaty of Guadalupe Hidalgo: A Legacy of Conflict*, Richard Griswold del Castillo successfully challenged the assertion that the U.S. victory brought liberty and peace to the conquered territory.[6] Thomas Hietala, Reginald Horsman, and Richard Slotkin all vigorously contested the dominant characterization of expansionism as a benign and positive movement. Instead, they argued that racism and violence stood at the core of the expansionist cause. These interpretations significantly differed from Albert K. Weinberg's 1935 book emphasizing both positive and negative aspects of Manifest Destiny.[7]

Ward McAfee and J. Cordell Robinson published translations of several crucial Mexican state documents that showed that nation's pre-war government to be very different from the swaggeringly belligerent one portrayed by Smith.[8] Pedro Santoni provided scholars with a history portraying some of the complex divisions within the Mexican polity and thereby added another dimension to our understanding of the conflict.[9]

The Mexican historiography of the 1846–48 conflict differs from that of the United States in several regards. While many U.S. officers and senior civilian officials published books about their wartime experiences, few of their counterparts across the Rio Grande did. The internally divisive elements of the 1846–48 struggle and the subsequent conflicts of the War of the Reforma seemed to have dampened the literary impulse of many leading Mexican figures of this period. Key persons such as Juan Álvarez, Anastasio Bustamante, Padre Dómeco Celedonio de Jarauta, Joaquín Rea, Juan Climaco Rebolledo, Juan Soto, and even Antonio López de Santa Anna himself did not leave detailed memoirs or extensive personal papers relating to the partisan movements or other aspects of the war.

Fortunately, a few Mexican officers left records of their experiences and impressions. These documents often are both forthright and interesting. In this genre, Lieutenant Manuel Balbontín's book merits mention.[10] This officer of the Mexican artillery force saw considerable service in the field and consequently wrote with the voice of authority and experience in describing such matters. He also understood the manner in which the Mexican government functioned and wrote with some eloquence and bitterness about the course and effect of such conduct.

Mexicans of letters and influence also wrote extensively about the conflict. The most important of these authors were often both scholars and participants in the great events of their time. Carlos María de Bustamante was one such person. A lawyer by training, he served México as a legislator, insurgent, and journalist. He wrote *El nuevo Bernal Diaz del Castillo, o sea, la historia de la invasion de los angloamericanos en México*.[11] In this book, he wove together extensive citations of primary sources, brief summaries of political and military events, chronologies, and essays. Regrettably, he completed the work before the final phases of the war, and this volume consequently lacks a review of that critical period.

Melchor Ocampo, a jurist, also contributed much to México's 1846–48 war effort as governor of Michoacán. In the days following the battle of Cerro Gordo, he wrote a fiery and eloquent plea calling upon the national government to wage guerrilla warfare against the invaders. His *Obras Completas* provides a valuable window to the great events of his time.[12] He opposed the Treaty of Guadalupe Hidalgo and subsequently served in Benito Juárez's cabinet following the triumph of the Plan of Ayutla.

Chihuahuan editor José Fernando Ramirez served México as a jurist, federal deputy, senator, and cabinet member. In 1848, he spoke before his fellow senators in favor of the peace treaty. Edited and published under the title of *México durante su guerra con los Estados Unidos*, his lengthy letters and other papers written during the war years provide a rare view of the thoughts and considerations of one of the nation's best minds.[13] Mariano Otero, another jurist, later worked as editor of the influential publication, *Siglo XIX*. In 1848, he joined with other federal deputies such as Benito Juárez and Manuel Cresencio Rejon in opposing the Treaty of Guadalupe Hidalgo.

Mexican historians who wrote in the years and decades following the war forswore adulatory biographies of senior officers and instead concentrated on producing narrative histories. Several works merit immediate mention. In the same year that the war ended, Ramón Alcaraz led a team of fifteen scholars that wrote a history focusing primarily upon the military aspects of the struggle. The members of the team produced a detailed and well-written narrative history, *Apuntes para la historia de la guerra entre México y los Estados Unidos.*[14] A U.S. veteran of the war, Colonel Albert C. Ramsey, deemed the work one whose "excellence will ensure for its authors a high celerity as men of taste, learning, and practical discrimination."[15]

However, the major nineteenth-century Mexican history of the war remains José María Roa Barcena's three-volume 1883 work, *Recuerdos de la invasión norteamericana, 1846–1848.* Barcena possessed an impressively broad and deep knowledge of the daily affairs of war and state as they unfolded during the conflict.[16] He included thousands of relevant details in the context of a lively narrative style. However, he shared with some of his American counterparts the habit of allowing cultural biases to interfere with his judgment.

Though U.S. historians continue to produce an impressive quantity of writing about the war, many of their works exhibit two weaknesses. First, they rely largely upon primary sources produced by their own countrymen. By following this course, they deny themselves a more detailed understanding of factors and perspectives governing the actions of the opposing side and of the interactions of the two nations at war. More importantly, U.S. historians of the conflict almost uniformly decline to address the expansionist movement in any framework other than the Manifest Destiny context. By doing so, these writers avoid discussing a subject that lies at the core of their country's history: the transformation of the United States of America from an Atlantic seaboard nation to a continental and then an inter-continental power.

However, some U.S. historians have indeed directly addressed this issue. They argue that Manifest Destiny existed not as a movement that ended in 1848, but as a set of beliefs that characterized their nation for much if not all of its history. Among those who advocate this perspective are R. W. Alstyne, Thomas R. Hietala, Myra Jehlen, Walter A. McDougall, Anders Stephanson, Albert K. Weinberg, and William Appleman Williams.[17]

Mexican historians of the 1846–48 conflict share with their American counterparts a propensity to view the expansionist movement primarily in the context of that war. Even those authors who examine the United States' armed interventions in their nation's affairs over a multi-century period do not offer a systemic and detailed survey of expansionism. For example, Gaston Garcia Cantu's *Las invasiones norteameicanas en México* provides a thorough examination of military encounters during the colonial, national, and modern periods while nonetheless treating the expansionist cause in a narrative rather than thematic context.[18]

Similarly, scholars in both nations, particularly those of the nineteenth century, often averted their gaze from the centuries-long intra-Mexican clash of culture, ethnicity, and power described in the first chapter of this book. For example, in their 1848 book, Ramón Alcaraz and his colleagues declared, "To explain then in a few words the true origin of the war, it is sufficient to say that the insatiable ambition of the United States, favored by our own weakness, caused it."[19] In turn, they attributed that weakness to disorder, personal egoism, and anarchy. Alcaraz and his co-authors did not undertake a systemic explanation of the processes that divided and weakened México in the decades preceding the outbreak of war.

José María Roa Barcena's 1883 work provided an explanation both different from and similar to that of Alcaraz and his colleagues. Like them, he cited standard causes such as weak political and social organization, "the poverty and exhaustion caused by twenty-five years of civil war, the failure of states to provide more aid to the national government, and inadequacies in the armed forces."[20] However, he also diverged from those standard explanations to blame the defeat on other causes.

His theories and his background merit mention. After a brief career in Jaliscan commerce, Roa Barcena (1827–1908) moved to Mexico City and began a lengthy career as a conservative man of letters. There, he founded and wrote for prominent rightist newspapers, accepted membership in Emperor Maximillian's Imperial Academy of Sciences and Literature, founded the Mexican Academy of Language, and then spent the years of the Porfiriato engaged in a wide range of literary activities.[21] In the spirit of Porfirians such as Senator Francisco Bulnes, he analyzed the 1846–48 war with the unselfconscious prejudice that marred so much of that era's Mexican historiography. Roa Barcena argued that the causes for the defeat also lay in México's "heterogeneity of races," in the "physical inferiority of races," and in diversion of resources to "suppress the Indians."[22] He took the veracity of his elitist beliefs for granted. The history produced by such authors invariably consigned the majority of their fellow citizens to the periphery. In this regard, Roa Barcena was the mirror image of Justin Smith. They both expressed their contempt for the persons of color who comprised the vast majority of México's people. That hostility between ruler and the ruled was far more damaging to México's prospects during the nineteenth century than any foreign invasion.

Happily, during recent decades the quality of writing about the war has improved in México just as it has in the United States. More than a century after Roa Barcena penned his assessments of the conflict, Joséfina Vásquez completed a splendidly broad and deep research effort for her 1997 history of this conflict. She concluded, "[Although] . . . the United States was politically and socially divided, . . . territorial ambition neutralized that polarization. The U.S. had resources, immigrants easily converted into volunteers, and a small but professional army equipped with modern armament. México lacked all of these. Also, the war and revolts had not only lessened the population's use for military service, but had demoralized them. The defeat was wholly predictable, without doubt, but perhaps the aftertaste would have been less bitter had the result been less resounding."[23] Further, she provided considerable evidence in support of her contention that México's system of government rendered the organization of a national defense difficult because "the ayuntamientos and the states, absorbed in their immediate problems, relegated the problem of the war to a secondary level."[24] Her conclusion accurately reflects one reality of that era.

Present-day Mexican scholars of the 1846–48 conflict exemplify a trend evident in other fields of their discipline: a shift toward regional and local histories. *México en guerra*, an anthology edited by Laura Herrera Serna, included twenty-six essays focusing on a particular aspect of the war in one specific state or city.[25] An additional five articles address broader subjects such as municipal finance during the war. By contrast, Maria Gayon Cordova's *La occupación yanqui de la ciudad de Mexico, 1847–1848* focuses upon a single city by relying extensively upon primary sources to discuss various aspects of life in the capital before, during, and after its fall.[26]

Given its tragic importance in Mexican history, the war continues to be a focus of much interest in that nation. In response, an interesting type of history book geared more toward the general reader than the professional historian has emerged. Typically, these books comprise no more than two hundred pages and do not include footnotes or indexes. In common with many scholarly works written on both sides of the border, they slight the deep issues raised by the partisan movement.

Those guerrilla forces posed an additional challenge to the prevailing interpretations of much of Mexican history. In the prevalent construct, the 1810–21 War of Independence forged a new nation. Yet in the 1840s, cleavages of culture, class, and race divided Mexican society more deeply than had been the case in the late colonial era. From the fall of Tenochtitlan until the Gríto de Dolores, no edict of the Spanish crown and no command of any viceroy ignited an indigenous rebellion equal in size or scope to 1846–49.

The dispossessed rebelled again and again. The revolts of 1846–49 represented only one link in a long series of such actions during the national period.[27] By assigning only marginal emphasis to these revolts, conservative historians created an inaccurate retelling of the past. In their versions of history, the key events and decisions take place within the small ranks of the literate, propertied, educated, and politically enabled minority who owned and operated most of México. The stories of those outside this circle become marginalized. In forcing their way to the center of the stage, the guerrilla combatants of 1846–49 compel us to reconsider the traditional remembrances of the past.

ARCHIVES CONSULTED

ACDN	Archivo de Cancelados de la Defensa Nacional, Mexico City
ADN	Folder section XI/481.3, Archivo de la Defensa Nacional, Mexico City
AGN	Ramo de Gobernación, Archivo General de la Nación, Mexico City
AHEM	Archivo Histórico del Estado México, Toluca, México
AHAO	Archivo Histórico del Ayuntamiento Orizaba, Orizaba, Veracruz
AHEO	Archivo Histórico del Estado de Oaxaca, Oaxaca
AHEV	Archivo Histórico del Estado de Veracruz, Xalapa
AHMX	Archivo Histórico del Municipio Xalapa, Veracruz
AHMT	Archivo Histórico Municipal de Toluca de Lerdo, México
AHSRE	Archivo Histórico de la Secretaría de Relaciones Exteriores, Mexico City
ASM	Archivo del Senado de México, Mexico City
BIM	Biblioteca Instituto Dr. José María Luis Mora, Mexico City
BLAC	Justin H. Smith Collection, Benson Latin American Collection, University of Texas, Austin
BMLT	Biblioteca Manuel Lerdo de Tejada, Mexico City
BNM	Banco Nacional de México, Mexico City
CEHM	Centro de Estudios de Historia de México (CONDUMEX), Mexico City
FRBN	Fondo Reservado y Biblioteca Nacional, Mexico City
GMWH	Ethan Allen Hitchcock Diary, Gilcrease Museum of Western History, Tulsa, Oklahoma
HNM	Hemeroteca Nacional de México, Mexico City
LCMSS	Library of Congress, Manuscripts Section, Washington, D.C.
MMOB	Mapoteca Manuel Orozco y Berra, Mexico City
NARA I	Records Group 94, National Archives and Records Administration, Washington, D.C.
NARA II	Records Group 59, National Archives and Records Administration, College Park, Maryland
USAMHI	Aztec Club Papers, United States Army Military History Institute, Carlisle, Pennsylvania

GOVERNMENT PUBLICATIONS

Contestaciones habides entre el supreme gobierno mexicano y el general en jefe del ejercito americano y el comissionado de los estados unidos. Mexico City: Imprenta de Vicente Garcia Torres, 1847.

Executive Document Number 1, Report of the Secretary of War to the Thirtieth Congress. Washington, D.C.: Wendell and Van Benthuysen, 1847.

Executive Document 56 of the House of Representatives: Messages from the President of the United States Transmitting Reports from the Secretary of State and the Secretary of War with Accompanying Documents in Compliance with the Resolution of the 7th February, 1848. Washington, D.C.: Wendell and Van Benthuysen, March 20, 1848.

Executive Document 59 of the House of Representatives: Message of the President of the United States Transmitting the Correspondence Between the Secretary of War and Major General Scott with the Accompanying Documents in Compliance with the Resolution of the House of the 7th Instant. Washington, D.C.: April 26, 1848.

Executive Documents Printed by Order of the Senate of the United States during the First Session of the Thirtieth Congress Begun and Held at the City of Washington, December 6, 1847, in Eight Volumes. Washington, D.C.: Wendell and Van Benthuysen, 1847.

Exposición con que el exmo. sr. ministro de hacienda a la camera de diputados en la sesión del día 9 de enero de 1849 el presupuesto general de gasta para el mismo año. Mexico City: Imprenta de Vicente G. Torres, 1849.

"Memoria de Hacienda, 1824–1825." Manuscript. Biblioteca Nacional de México, Archivo General de la Nación, Mexico City.

Memoria de la hacienda federal de los estados unidos mexicanos, presentada al congreso general de la unión por el secretario del ramo en 22 de mayo de 1835. Mexico City: Imprenta de Aguila, 1835.

Memoria de la hacienda nacional de la republica mexicana presentada a las cameras del ministro del ramo en julio de 1840. Mexico City: Imprenta de Aguila, 1841.

Memoria de la hacienda nacional de la republica mexicana presentada a las cameras del ministro del ramo en julio de 1846, primera parte. Mexico City: Imprenta de Ignacio Cumplido, 1846.

Memoria de la hacienda nacional de la republica mexicana presentada a las cameras por el ministero del ramo en julio de 1839. Mexico City: Imprenta de Aguila, 1840.

Memoria de la hacienda nacional de la republica mexicana presentada a las cameras por el ministro del ramo en julio de 1838, segunda parte. Mexico City: Imprenta de Aguila, 1838.

Memoria del ministerio de estado y del despache de guerra y marina del gobierno supremo de la republica mexicana leida al augusto congreso nacional el día 9 de diciembre de 1846 por el general Almonte. Mexico City: Imprenta de Torres, 1846.

Memoria del ministro de hacienda de la republica mexicana presentado por el secretario del ramo en febrero de 1850. Mexico City, 1850.

Memoria del ramo de hacienda federal de los estados unidos mexicanos leida en la camera de diputados el 13 de enero en la de senadores al 16 del mismo, por el ministro respectivo año de 1826. Mexico City: Imprenta de Supremo Gobierno, 1826.

Memoria del ramo de la hacienda federal de los estados unidos mexicanos leida en la camera de diputados por el ministro respectivo el día 3 y en la de senadores el 7 de enero de 1829. Mexico City: Imprenta de Aguila, 1829.

Memoria del ramo de la hacienda federal de los estados unidos mexicanos leida por el encargado del ministerio respectivo en la camera de senadores el 1 y en la de diputados el 7 de febrero de 1828. Mexico City: Imprenta del Supremo Gobierno, 1828.

Memoria del secretario del despacho de hacienda leida en la camera de senadores de día 15 y en la de diputados el 17 de febrero de 1832. Mexico City: Imprenta de Aguila, 1832.

Memoria del secretario del estado y del despacho de guerra y marina leide en la camera de diputados el día 9 y en la de senadores el 11 de enero de 1849. Mexico City, 1849.

Memoria nacional de la hacienda de la republica mexicana a las cameras por el ministro del ramo en julio de 1849. Mexico City: Imprenta de Aguila, 1849.

Memoria que sobre el estado de la hacienda nacional de la republica mexicana presentada a las cameras por el ministro del ramo en julio de 1845. Mexico City: Imprenta de Ignacio Cumplido, 1846.

Polk, James K. *Message from the President of the United State to the Two Houses of Congress at the Commencement of the First Session of the Thirtieth Congress, December 7, 1847.* Washington, D.C.: Van Benthuysen, 1847.

Senate Executive Document No. 36, 30th Congress, 1st Session, Report of the Secretary of War Showing the Number of Troops in the Service of the United States in México since the Commencement of the War, Killed, Wounded, Etc. Washington, D.C.: Wendell and Van Benthuysen, 1848.

United States War Department, *Instruction for Field Artillery: Horse and Foot.* Baltimore: Joseph Robinson, 1845.

SPEECHES

Bowlin, J. W. *Speech of the Honorable J. W. Bowlin of Missouri Delivered in the House of Representatives, December 24, 1846.* Washington, D.C.: Blair and Rives, 1846.

Culver, E. D. *Old Federalism & Modern Democracy. Speech of Hon. E. D. Culver of New York on the Mexican War.* Washington, D.C.: J. & G.S. Gideon Printers, 1847.

Hale, J. P. *Speech of J. P. Hale of New Hampshire on the Increase of the Army in México Delivered in the Senate of the United States, January 6, 1848.* Washington, D.C.: Tower Printers, 1848.

Jameson, John. *Speech of the Hon. John Jameson of Missouri on the War with México Delivered in the House of Representatives Tuesday, January 18, 1848.* Washington, D.C., 1848.

King, Donald P. *Speech of Mr. Donald P. King of Massachusetts on the General Appropriation Bill and the Mexican War, Delivered February 4, 1847.* Washington, D.C.: J. & G. S. Gideon, 1847.

Tibbatts, J. W. *Speech of the Honorable J. W. Tibbatts of Kentucky in the House of Representatives, January 8, 1847.* Washington, D.C.: Blair and Rives, 1847.

NEWSPAPERS

The American Star, 1847–48. Veracruz. Hemeroteca Nacional de México, Mexico City.

El Diario del Gobierno, 1835, 1838, 1847. Mexico City. Hemeroteca Nacional de México, Mexico City.

El Siglo XIX, 1847–48. Mexico City. Hemeroteca Nacional de México, Mexico City.

El Republicano, 1847–48. Mexico City. Hemeroteca Nacional de México, Mexico City.

BOOKS, ARTICLES, AND DISSERTATIONS

Adams, Henry. *The Life of Albert Gallatin.* New York: Peter Smith, 1943.

Alamán, Lucas. *Historia de México.* Mexico City: Editoria Jus, 1942.

Alcaraz, Ramón, ed. *Apuntes para la historia de la guerra entre México y los estados unidos*. 1848. Reprint, Mexico City: Siglo Vientiuno Editores, 1970.

_____, ed. *The Other Side: or Notes for the History of the War between México and the United States*. Translated by Albert C. Ramsey. New York: John Wiley, 1850.

Álvarez, Daniel Molina. *La passion de padre Jarauta*. Mexico City: Gobierno de la Ciudad de Mexico, 1999.

Anderson, Robert. *An Artillery Officer in the Mexican War 1846–7: Letters of Robert Anderson, Captain 3RD Artillery, U.S.A.* New York: G. P. Putnam's Sons, 1911.

Anna, Timothy E. *The Fall of the Royal Government in Mexico City*. Lincoln: University of Nebraska Press, 1978.

Arnold, Linda. *Bureaucracy and Bureaucrats in Mexico City 1742–1835*. Tucson: University of Arizona Press, 1988.

Baker, George Towne, III. "Mexico City and the War with the United States: A Study in the Politics of Military Occupation." Ph.D., diss., Duke University, 1970.

Balbontín, Mañuel. *La invasion americana: apuntes de subteniente de artilleria Mañuel Balbontín*. Mexico City: Tipografía de Gonzalo A. Esteva, 1888.

Ballantine, George. *The Mexican War by an English Soldier Comprising Incidents and Adventures in the United States and México with the American Army*. New York: W. A. Townsend & Company, 1860.

Bartlett, John. *Bartlett's Familiar Quotations*. Boston: Little, Brown, 1980.

Batalla, Guillermo Bonfil. *México Profundo: Reclaiming a Civilization*. Translated by Philip A. Dennis. Austin: University of Texas Press, 1996.

Bauer, K. Jack. *The Mexican War 1846–1848*. New York: Macmillan Publishing Company, Inc., 1974.

_____. *Surfboats and Horse Marines: U.S. Naval Operations in the Mexican War, 1846–1848*. Annapolis: United States Naval Institute Press, 1969.

Baylies, Francis. *A Narrative of Major General Wool's Campaign in México in the Years 1846, 1847, and 1848*. 1851. Reprint, Austin: Jenkins Publishing Company, 1975.

Bazant, Jan. *A Concise History of México from Hidalgo to Cardenas 1805–1940*. London: Cambridge University Press, 1977.

Beauregard, P. G. T. *With Beauregard in México: The Mexican War Reminiscences of P. G. T. Beauregard*. Edited by Harry T. Williams. Baton Rouge: Louisiana State University Press, 1956.

Benson, Nettie Lee. *The Provincial Deputation in Mexico*. Austin: University of Texas Press, 1955.

Bill, Alfred Hoyt. *Rehearsal for Conflict: The War with México 1846–1848*. New York: Cooper Square Publishers, Inc., 1969.

Bodson, Robert L. "A Description of the United States Occupation of México as Reported by American Newspapers Published in Veracruz, Puebla and Mexico City September 14, 1847, to July 31, 1848." Ph.D. diss., Ball State University, 1971.

Borah, Woodrow, and Sherburne P. Cook. "The Aboriginal Population of Central México on the Eve of the Spanish Conquest." *Ibero-Americana* 45 (1963): 72–94.

Brack, Gene M. *México Views Manifest Destiny 1821–1846*. Albuquerque: University of New Mexico Press, 1975.

Brackett, Albert G. *General Lane's Brigade in México*. Cincinnati: H. W. Derby & Co. and New York: J. C. Derby, 1854.

Breithaupt, Richard Hoag, Jr. *Aztec Club of 1847: Military Society of the Mexican War Sesquicentennial History*. Los Angeles: Wilika Publishing Company, 1998.

Brooks, Nathan Covington. *A Complete History of the Mexican War: Its Causes, Conduct, and Consequences*. Philadelphia: Grigg, Elliot & Co., 1849.

Bushnell, Clyde G. "The Political and Military Career of Juan Álvarez, 1790–1867." Ph.D. diss., University of Texas, 1958.

Bustamante, Carlos María de. *El nuevo Bernal Diaz del Castillo, o sea, historia de la invasión de los angloamericanos en México*. 1847. Reprint, Mexico City: Consejo nacional para la cultura y las artes, 1997.

Cantu, Gaston Garcia. *La intervención norteamericana en México*. Mexico City: Ediciones Era, 1971.

Caraza, Leopoldo Martinez. *La intervención norteamericana en México, 1846–1848*. Mexico City: Panorama Editorial, 1981.

Casas, Bartolome de las. *A Short Account of the Destruction of the Indies*. London: Penguin Books, 1992.

Castillo, Richard Griswold del. *The Treaty of Guadalupe Hidalgo: A Legacy of Conflict*. Norman: University of Oklahoma Press, 1990.

Castro, Miguel Medina. *El gran despojo: Tejas, Nuevo México y California*. Mexico City: Editorial Diogenes, S.A., 1974.

Cesar, José Manuel Villalpondo. *Las balas del invasor: la expansion territorial de los Estados Unidos a costa de México*. Mexico City: Amargur, 1998.

Chamberlain, Samuel. *My Confession: Recollections of a Rogue*. Edited by William H. Goetzmann. Austin: Texas State Historical Association, 1996.

Chance, Joseph E. *Jefferson Davis' Mexican War Regiment*. Jackson: University of Mississippi Press, 1991.

_____, ed. and annotator. *Mexico under Fire, Being the Diary of Samuel Ryan Curtis, 3rd Ohio Volunteer Regiment, during the American Military Occupation of Northern Mexico, 1846-1847*. Fort Worth: Texas Christian University Press, 1994.

Clausewitz, Carl von. *On War*. Princeton: Princeton University Press, 1976.

Coatsworth, John H. "Measuring Influence," in *Rural Revolt in México: U.S. Intervention and the Domain of Subaltern Politics*, edited by Daniel Nugent. Durham: Duke University Press, 1988.

Condor, Seymour, and Odie B. Faulk. *North America Divided: The Mexican American War 1846–1847*. New York: Oxford University Press, 1971.

Cordova, Maria Gayon, ed. *La ocupación yanqui de la ciudad de Mexico, 1847–1848*. Mexico City: Consejo Nacional para la Cultura y las Artes and the Instituto Nacional de Antropología e Historia, 1997.

Cortés, Fernando (Hernán). *Letters from Mexico*. New York: Grossman, 1971.

Cortes, Raul Arreola, ed. *Obras completas de don Melchor Ocampo: documentos politicos y familiares, 1842–1851*. Morelia, México: Comité Editorial del Gobierno de Michoacán, 1986.

Costeloe, Michael P. *La primera republica federal de México (1824–1835)*. Mexico City: Fonda de la Cultura Económica, 1975.

_____. *The Central Republic in México, 1835–1846*. New York: Cambridge University Press, 1993.

Denevan, William M., ed. *The Native Population of the Americas in 1492*. Madison: University of Wisconsin Press, 1976.

DePalo, William A. *The Mexican National Army, 1822–1852*. College Station: Texas A&M University Press, 1997.

_____. Email to author, 19 April 1998.

Diaz Diaz, Fernando. *Caudillos y caciques: Antonio López de Santa Anna y Juan Álvarez*. Mexico City: El Colegio de México, 1972.

Diccionario porrúa de historia, biografía y geografía de México. 4 vols. Mexico City: Editorial Porrúa, S.A., 1995.

Dillon, Lester R. *American Artillery in the Mexican War, 1846–1848*. Austin: Presidial Press, 1975.

DiTella, Torcuato S. *National Popular Politics in Early Independent México, 1820–1847*. Albuquerque: University of New Mexico Press, 1996.

Downey, Joseph T. *The Cruise of the Portsmouth, 1845–1847: A Sailor's View of the Naval Conquest of California*. 1848. Reprint, New Haven: Yale University Press, 1982.

Drexler, Robert. *Guilty of Making Peace: A Biography of Nicholas P. Trist*. New York: University Press of America, 1991.

Earle, Rebecca, ed. *Rumours of Wars: Civil Conflict in Nineteenth-Century Latin America*. London: Institute of Latin American Studies, 2000.

Edwards, Sherman, and Peter Stone. *1776: A Musical Play*. New York: Viking Press, 1970.

Eisenhower, John S. D. *So Far from God: The U.S. War with México 1846–1848*. New York: Random House, 1869.

Esposito, Vincent J., ed. *The West Point Atlas of American Wars, Volume 1, 1689–1900*. New York: Henry Holt & Company, 1995.

Estrada, Genaro, and Carlos Pereyra. *México durante la guerra con los Estados Unidos*. Mexico City: Librería de Ch. Bouret, 1905.

Fehrenbach, T. H. *Lone Star: A History of Texas and the Texans*. New York: American Legacy Press, 1968.

_____. *Fire & Blood: A History of México*. New York: Da Capo Press, 1995.

Feldberg, Michael. *The Turbulent Era: Riot and Disorder in Jacksonian America*. New York: Oxford University Press, 1980.

Ferrell, Robert H., ed. *Monterrey Is Ours! The Mexican War Letters of Lieutenant Dana 1845–1847*. Louisville: The University Press of Kentucky, 1990.

Florescano, Enrique. *Memory, Myth, and Time in México: From the Aztecs to Independence*. Austin: University of Texas Press, 1994.

Fodor's 1996 Guide to Mexico. Edited by Edie Jaolim. New York: Fodor's Publications, 1995.

Foos, Paul. *A Short, Offhand Killing Affair: Soldiers and Social Conflict during the Mexican-American War*. Chapel Hill: University of North Carolina Press, 2002.

Fowler, Will. *Tornel and Santa Anna: The Writer and the Caudillo, México, 1795–1853*. Westport, Conn.: Greenwood Press, 2000.

Francaviglia, Richard V., and Douglas E. Richmond, eds. *Dueling Eagles: Reinterpreting the U.S.-Mexican War, 1846–1848*. Fort Worth: Texas Christian University Press, 2000.

Frias, Heriberto. *Episodios militares mexicanos*. Mexico City: Secretaría de la Defensa Nacional, 1983.

Frost, John L. *The Mexican War and Its Warriors*. New Haven, Conn.: H. Mansfield, 1848.

_____. *The History of México and Its Wars*. New Orleans: Armand Hawkins, 1882.

Fuller, John Douglas Pitts. *The Movement for the Acquisition of All México 1846–1848*. Baltimore: The Johns Hopkins Press, 1936.

_____. "The Slavery Question and the Movement to Acquire México 1846–1848." *The Mississippi Valley Historical Review* 21, no. 1 (June 1934): 31–48.

Galeana, Patricia, ed. *En defensa de la patria*. Mexico City: Secretaría de Gobernación, 1997.

_____. *El nacimiento de México*. Mexico City: Fondo de Cultura Económica, 1999.

Gallatin, Albert. *Expenses of the War*. Washington, D.C.: J. Tower Printers, 1848.

García, Carlos Bosch. *La historia de las relaciones entre México y los Estados Unidos, 1819–1848*. Mexico City: Escuela Nacional de Ciencias Políticas, 1961.

Garfias, M. Luis. *Guerrilleros of México: Famous Historical Figures and Their Exploits from Independence to the Mexican Revolution*. Mexico City: Panorama Editorial, 1980.

Garner, Mark L., and Marc Simmons, eds. *The Mexican War Correspondence of Richard Elliott Smith*. Norman: University of Oklahoma Press, 1997.

Gaxiola, Francisco Javier. *Gobernantes del estado de México: Muzquiz-Zavala-Olaguibel*. 1899. Reprint, Mexico City: Mario Colin, 1975.

Ghizliazza, Mestre. *Invasión norteamericano en Tabasco*. Mexico City: Documentos Consejo Editorial del Gobierno del Estado de Tabasco, Imprenta Universitaria, 1948.

Gibson, Charles. *The Aztecs Under Spanish Rule: A History of the Indians of the Valley of México, 1519–1810*. Palo Alto: Stanford University Press, 1964.

Gilje, Paul A. *The Road to Mobocracy: Popular Disorder in New York, 1763–1834*. Chapel Hill: University of North Carolina Press, 1987.

Griswold del Castillo, Richard. *The Treaty of Guadalupe-Hidalgo*. Norman: University of Oklahoma Press, 1990.

Guardino, Peter. "Barbarism or Republican Law? Guerrero's Peasants and National Politics, 1820–1846." *Hispanic American Historical Review* 75, no. 2 (1995): 185–203.

_____. *Peasants, Politics, and the Formation of México's National State: Guerrero, 1800–1857*. Palo Alto: Stanford University Press, 1996.

Hackenburg, Randy. *Pennsylvania in the War with México: The Volunteer Regiments*. Shippensburg, Pa.: White Mane Publishing Company, 1992.

Halleck, Henry W. *The Mexican War in Baja California: The Memorandum of Captain Henry W. Halleck Concerning His Expeditions in Lower California*. Edited by Nunis B. Doyce. Los Angeles: Dawson's Book Shop, 1977.

Hanke, Lewis. *Aristotle and the American Indians: A Study in Race Prejudice in the Modern World*. Chicago: Henry Regnery Company, 1959.

Heering, Patricia Roche. *General José Cosme Urrea: His Life and Times*. Spokane, Wash.: Arthur H. Clarke Company, 1995.

Heintzelman, Captain Samuel P. S. P. Heintzelman Journal, 1847–1850. Library of Congress, Manuscripts Section, Washington, D.C.

Henry, W. S. *Campaign Sketches of the War with México*. New York: Harper & Brothers Publishers, 1847.

Hietala, Thomas R. *Manifest Destiny: Anxious Aggrandizement in Late Jacksonian America*. Ithaca, N.Y.: Cornell University Press, 1995.

Hobsbawm, Eric J. *Social Bandits and Primitive Rebels: Studies of Archaic Forms of Social Movements in the 19th and 20th Centuries*. Glencoe, Ill.: The Free Press, 1959.

Horsman, Reginald. *Race and Manifest Destiny: The Origins of American Racial Anglo-Saxonism*. Cambridge: Harvard University Press, 1981.

Humboldt, Alexander von. *Political Essay on the Kingdom of New Spain*. New York: Alfred A. Knopf, 1972.

Jehlen, Myra. *American Incarnation: The Individual, the Nation, and the Continent*. Cambridge, Mass.: Harvard University Press, 1986.

Jenkins, John S. *History of the War Between the United States and México from the Commencement of Hostilities to the Ratification of the Treaty of Peace*. New York: Derby Miller & Company, 1850.

Jennings, Francis. *The Founders of America: How Indians Discovered the Land, Pioneered in It, and Created A Great Classical Civilization, How They Were Plunged into A Dark Age by Invasion and Conquest, and How They Are Reviving*. New York: W. W. Norton & Company, 1993.

Johannsen, Robert J. *To the Halls of the Montezumas: The Mexican War in the American Imagination*. New York: Oxford University Press, 1985.

Johnson, Timothy D. *Winfield Scott: The Quest for Military Glory*. Lawrence: University of Kansas Press, 1998.

Jomini, Antoine Henri. *The Life of Napoleon*. Translated by Henry W. Halleck. New York: D. Van Nostrand, 1864.

Jordan, H. Donaldson. "A Politician of Expansion: Robert J. Walker." *The Mississippi Valley Historical Review* 19, no. 2 (December 1932): 362–81.

Kahle, Gunter. *El ejercito y la formación del estado en los comienzos de la independencia de México*. Mexico City: Fondo de Cultura Económica, 1997.

Katz, Friedrich, ed. *Riot, Rebellion, and Revolution: Rural and Social Conflict in México*. Princeton: Princeton University Press, 1988.

_____. *The Life and Times of Pancho Villa*. Palo Alto: Stanford University Press, 1998.

Kenly, John Reese. *Memoirs of Maryland Volunteer: War with México in the Years 1846–1848*. Philadelphia: J. B. Lippincott & Company, 1873.

Ker, Anita Melville. *Mexican Government Publications: A Guide to the More Important Publications of the National Government of México, 1821–1936*. Washington, D.C.: United States Government Printing Office, 1940.

Kuppenheimer, L. B. *Albert Gallatin's Vision of Democratic Stability: An Interpretive Profile*. Westport, Conn.: Praeger Publishers, 1996.

Ladd, Horatio O. *History of the War with México*. New York: Dodd, Mead & Company, 1882.

Lander, Ernest McPherson, Jr. *Reluctant Imperialists: Calhoun, the South Carolinians, and the Mexican War*. Baton Rouge: Louisiana State University Press, 1980.

Landis, J. F. Reynolds. *Constitution of the Aztec Club of 1847 and a List of Members*. London: Hanburry, Tomsett & Co., 1928.

Leon, Arnoldo de. *They Called Them Greasers: Anglo Attitudes towards Mexicans in Texas, 1821–1900*. Austin: University of Texas Press, 1983.

Livermore, Abiel Abott. *War with México Reviewed*. Boston: J. D. Flagg and W. H. Hardwell, 1850.

Livingston-Little, D. E., ed. *The Mexican War Diary of Thomas D. Tennery.* Norman: University of Oklahoma Press, 1970.

Logan, John Alexander. *The Volunteer Soldier of America: With Memoirs of the Author and Military Reminiscences from General Logan's Private Journal.* Chicago: R. S. Peale & Company, 1887.

Lopez y Rivas, Gilberto. *La guerra del 47 y las resistencia popular a la ocupación.* Mexico City: Editorial Nuestra Tiempo, 1976.

Lynch, John. *Caudillos in Spanish America 1800–1850.* Oxford, U.K.: Clarendon Press, 1992.

_____. *The Spanish-American Revolutions, 1808–1826.* New York: W. W. Norton & Company, 1973.

Malone, Dumas, and Basil Rauch. *Empire for Liberty: The Genesis and Growth of the United States of America.* New York: Appleton-Century Crofts, Inc., 1960.

Manning, William R. *Early Diplomatic Relations Between México and the United States.* New York: Greenwood Publishers, 1968.

_____. *Diplomatic Correspondence of the United States: Inter-American Affairs, 1831–1860.* Washington, D.C.: Carnegie Endowment for International Peace, 1937.

Mansfield, Edward D. *The Mexican War: A History of Its Origins.* New York: A. S. Barnes & Company, 1850.

_____. *Life and Services of General Winfield Scott, Including the Siege of Veracruz, the Battle of Cerro Gordo, and the Battles in the Valley of México: To the Conclusion of Peace and His Return to the United States.* New York: A. S. Barnes & Co., 1842.

Mantecon, María del Carmen Vasquez. *La palabra del poder: Vida pública de José María Tornel y Mendivil (1795–1853).* Mexico City: Universidad nacional autonoma de México, 1997.

Martinez, Orlando. *The Great Land Grab.* London: Quartet Books, 1975.

May, Robert E. *John A. Quitman: Old South Crusader.* Baton Rouge: Louisiana State University Press, 1985.

McAfee, Ward, and J. Cordell Robinson, eds. *Origins of the Mexican War: A Documentary Source Book.* Salisbury, N.C.: Documentary Publications, 1982.

McCaffrey, James M., ed. *Surrounded by Dangers of All Kinds: The Mexican War Letters of Lieutenant Theodore Laidley.* Denton: University of North Texas Press, 1997.

_____. *Army of Manifest Destiny: The American Soldier in the Mexican War, 1846–1848.* New York: University Press, 1992.

McClellan, George B. *The Mexican War Diary of General George B. McClellan,* edited by William Starr Myers. Princeton: Princeton University Press, 1917.

McDougall, Walter A. *Promised Land, Crusader State: The American Encounter with the World Since 1776.* Boston: Houghton Mifflin Company, 1997.

Meyer, Brantz. *History of the War Between the United States and México.* New York: Wiley & Putnam, 1848.

Meyer, Michael C., and William L. Sherman, *The Course of Mexican History.* New York: Oxford University Press, 1995.

Miller, Robert Ryal, ed. *The Mexican War Journal and Letters of Ralph W. Kirkham.* College Station: Texas A&M University Press, 1991.

Mora, José María Luis. *Ensayos, ideas, y retratos.* Mexico City: Universidad Nacional Autonoma de Mexico, 1941.

Morison, Samuel Elliot. *"Old Bruin": Commodore Matthew Calbraith Perry, 1794–1858*. Boston: Little, Brown and Company, 1967.

Moseley, Edward H., and Paul C. Clark, Jr. *Historical Dictionary of the United States–Mexican War: Wars, Revolution, and Civil Unrest*. Lanham, Md.: The Scarecrow Press, Inc., 1997.

Muller, John. *A Treatise of Artillery*. 1780. Reprint, Bloomfield, Ontario: Museum Restoration Service, 1977.

Negrete, Emilio del Castillo. *Invasión de los norte-americanos*. Mexico City: Imprenta del Editor, 1890.

O, Jaime E. Rodriguez, ed. *México in the Age of Democratic Revolutions*. Boulder: Lynne Reiner Publishers, Inc., 1994.

Ocampo, Melchor. *Obras completas de don Melchor Ocampo, tomo III*. Morelia, México: Comite Editorial del Gobierno de Michoacán, 1986.

Ohrt, Wallace. *Defiant Peacemaker: Nicholas Trist in the Mexican War*. College Station: Texas A&M University Press, 1997.

Oswandel, Jacob J. *Notes of the Mexican War, 1846–1847–1848*. Philadelphia, 1885.

Otero, Mariano, *Obras—Tomo II*. Edited by Jesus Reyes Heroles. Mexico City: Editorial Porrúa, 1967.

Oxford Dictionary of Quotations, third edition. New York: Oxford University Press, 1979.

Padden, R. C. *The Hummingbird and the Hawk: Conquest and Sovereignty in the Valley of México*. New York: Harper Torchbooks, 1967.

Paz, Eduardo. *La invasión norte-americana en 1846: ensayo de historia patria-militar por el mayor de caballero*. Mexico City: Imprenta Moderna de Carlos Paz, 1889.

Peck, John James. *The Sign of the Eagle: A View of México—1830 to 1855: The descriptive and poignant letters of Lieutenant John James Peck, a United States soldier in the conflict with México, and the enchanting color lithographs of México by John Phillips, Carl Nebel, Daniel Thomas Egerton, Casimiro Castro, and Captain P. D. Whitney*. San Diego: Union Tribune Publishing Company, 1970.

Peskin, Allan, ed. *Volunteers: The Mexican War Journals of Private Richard Coulter and Sergeant Thomas Barclay, Company E, Second Pennsylvania Infantry*, Kent, Ohio: Kent State University Press, 1991.

Pletcher, David M. *The Diplomacy of Annexation: Texas, Oregon, and the Mexican War*. Columbia: University of Missouri Press, 1973.

Pohl, James W. "The Influence of Antoine Henri Jomini on Winfield Scott's Campaign in the Mexican War." *Southwestern Historical Quarterly* 67 (1973–74): 85–110.

Polk, James K. *The Diary of a President, 1845–1849*. Edited by Allan Nevins. New York: Longmans, Green & Company, 1952.

_____. *The Diary of James K. Polk during his Presidency*. Edited by Milo Milton Quaife. Chicago: A. C. McClurg & Co., 1910.

Pratt, Julius W. "The Origin of "Manifest Destiny." *The Mississippi Valley Historical Review* 32, no. 2 (July 1927): 795–98.

Ramirez, José Fernando. *México durante su guerra con los Estados Unidos*. Mexico City: Vda de C. Bouret, 1905.

_____. *México during the War with the United States*. Edited by Walter V. Scholes. Translated by Elliot B. Scherr. Columbia: University of Missouri Press, 1950.

Reed, Nelson A. *The Caste War of Yucatán*. Palo Alto: Stanford University Press, 2001.

Reeves, Jesse S. *American Diplomacy under Tyler and Polk*. Gloucester, Mass.: Peter Smith, 1967.

Reina, Leticia. *Las rebeliones campesinas en México, 1819–1906*. Mexico City: Siglo Vientiuno, 1980.

Rejon, Manuel Crescencio. "Observation of the Treaty of Guadalupe Hidalgo." In *The View from Chapultepec–Mexican Writers on the Mexican-American War*, edited by Cecil Robinson. Tucson: The University of Arizona Press, 1989.

Remini, Robert V. *Henry Clay: Statesman for the Union*. New York: W. W. Norton & Company, 1991.

Rives, George Lockhart. *The United States and México*. New York: Charles Scribner's Sons, 1913.

Roa Barcena, José María. *Recuerdos de la invasión norteamericana: 1846–1848*. Mexico City: Editorial Porrúa, S.A., 1971.

Robinson, Cecil, ed. *The View from Chapultepec: Mexican Writers on the Mexican-American War*. Tucson: University of Arizona Press, 1989.

Robinson, Jacob S. *A Journal of the Santa Fe Expedition under Colonel Doniphan*. 1848. Reprint, New York: Da Capo Press, 1972.

Robles, Vito Alessio. *Guia del archivo histórico militar de México: Formada del orden de la dirección archivo miltar, Tomo I y II*. Mexico City: Taller Autografia, 1948.

Santa Anna, Antonio López de, et al. *The Mexican Side of the Texas Revolution*. Translated by Carlos Castañeda. Dallas: P. L. Turner Company, 1928.

Santoni, Pedro. *Mexicans at Arms: Puro Federalists and the Politics of War, 1845–1848*. Fort Worth: Texas Christian University Press, 1996.

Saxton, Alexander. *The Rise and Fall of the White Republic: Class Politics and Mass Culture in Nineteenth-Century America*. New York: Verso, 1990.

Schoular, James. *History of the United States under the Constitution*. 1908. Reprint, New York: Kraus Reprint Company, 1970.

Schroeder, John H. *Mr. Polk's War: American Opposition and Dissent, 1846–1848*. Madison: University of Wisconsin Press, 1973.

Schultz, Eric B., and Michael J. Tougias. *King Philip's War: The History and Legacy of America's Forgotten Conflict*. Woodstock, Vt.: The Countryman Press, 1999.

Scott, Winfield. *Memoirs of Lieut.-General Scott, LL.D*. New York: Sheldon & Company, 1864.

Scribner, Benjamin Franklin. *A Campaign in México or A Glimpse at Life in the Camp*. 1847. Reprint, Austin: Jenkins Publishing Company, 1995.

Selby, John. *The Eagle and the Serpent: The Spanish and American Invasions of México, 1519 and 1846*. London: Hamish Hamilton, 1978.

Serna, Laura Herrera, ed. *México en guerra (1846–1848): perspectivas regionales*. Mexico City: Consejo Nacional para la Cultura y las Artes and the Museo Nacional de las Intervenciones, 1997.

Shenton, James P. *Robert John Walker: A Politician from Jackson to Lincoln*. New York: Columbia University Press, 1961.

Sierra, Justo. *The Political Evolution of the Mexican People*. Austin: University of Texas Press, 1969.

Sims, Harold Dana. *The Expulsion of México's Spaniards, 1821–1836*. Pittsburgh, Pa.: University of Pittsburgh Press, 1990.

Smart, Charles Allen. *Viva Juárez: A Biography.* Philadelphia: Lippincott, 1963.

Smith, Ephraim Kirby. *To México with Scott: Letters of Captain E. Kirby Smith to His Wife.* Cambridge: Harvard University Press, 1917.

Smith, George Winston, and Charles Judah, eds. *Chronicles of the Gringos: The U.S. Army in the Mexican War, 1846–1848, Accounts of Eyewitnesses and Combatants.* Albuquerque: University of New Mexico Press, 1968.

Smith, Gustavus. *Company "A" Corps of Engineers, U.S.A., 1846–1848 in the Mexican War.* Willets Point, N.Y.: The Battalion Press, 1896.

Smith, Howard R. *Economic History of the United States.* New York: Ronald Press Company, 1955.

Smith, Justin H. *The War with México, Volumes I and II.* 1919. Reprint, Gloucester, Mass.: Peter Smith, 1963.

Smith, Peter H. *Talons of the Eagle: Dynamics of U.S.-Latin American Relations.* New York: Oxford University Press, 1996.

Sobarzo, Alejandro. *Deber y Conciencia: Nicolas Trist el negociador norteamericano el la guerra del 47.* Mexico City: Editorial Diana 1990.

Stannard, David E. *American Holocaust: Columbus and the Conquest of the New World.* New York: Oxford University Press, 1992.

Stephanson, Anders. *Manifest Destiny: American Expansionism and the Empire of Right.* New York: Hill and Wang, 1995.

Stephenson, Nathaniel W. *Texas and the Mexican War: A Chronicle of the Winning of the Southwest.* New Haven: Yale University Press, 1921.

Stevens, Donald Fithian. *Origins of Instability in Early Republican México.* Durham, N.C.: Duke University Press, 1991.

Taylor, Zachary. *Letters of Zachary Taylor from the Battle-fields of the Mexican War.* 1908. Reprint, New York: Kraus Reprint Company, 1970.

TePaske, John. "The Financial Disintegration of the Royal Government of México during the Epoch of Independence." In *The Independence of México and the Creation of the New Nation.* Los Angeles: UCLA Latin American Publications, 1989.

Thompson, Waddy. *Recollections of México.* New York: Wiley and Putnam, 1846.

Thomson, Guy P. C., and Davis G. LaFrance. *Patriots, Politics, and Popular Liberalism in Nineteenth-Century México: Juan Francisco Lucas and the Puebla Sierra.* Wilmington, Del.: Scholarly Resources, Inc, 1999.

Tornel y Mendívil, José María. *Breve resena historia de los acontecimientos mas notable de la nación mexicana.* Mexico City: Instituto Nacional de Estudios Históricos de la Revolución Mexicana, 1985.

Turner, Frederick C. *The Dynamics of Mexican Nationalism.* Chapel Hill: University of North Carolina Press, 1968.

Tutorow, Norman. *The Mexican-American War: An Annotated Bibliography.* Westport, Conn.: Greenwood Press, 1981.

Ugarte, Manuel. *The Destiny of a Continent.* 1925. Reprint, New York: AMS Press, 1970.

Valades, José C. *Breve historia de la guerra con los Estados Unidos.* Mexico City: Editorial Diana, 1980.

Van Alstyne, R. W. *The Rising American Empire.* New York: Oxford University Press, 1960.

Vásquez, Joséfina Zoraida. *La intervención norteamericana, 1846–1848.* Mexico City: Secretaría de Relaciones Exteriores, 1997.

_____, ed. *México al tiempo de su guerra con los estados unidos (1846–1848)*. Mexico City: Secretaría de Relaciones Exteriores and the Fondo de Cultura Económica, 1997.

_____, and Lorenzo Meyer. *México frente a los Estados Unidos*. Mexico City: Secretaría de Relaciones Exteriores and the Fondo de Cultura Económica, 1982.

Warren, Richard A. *Vagrants and Citizens: Politics and the Masses in Mexico City from Colony to Republic*. Wilmington, Del.: Scholarly Resources Press, 2001.

Weber, David M. *The Mexican Frontier, 1821–1846*. Albuquerque: University of New Mexico Press, 1982.

Weems, John Edward. *To Conquer a Peace: The War between the United States and México*. College Station: Texas A&M University Press, 1974.

Weinberg, Albert K. *Manifest Destiny: A Study of Nationalist Expansion in American History*. Baltimore: The Johns Hopkins University Press, 1935.

Wilcox, Cadmus M. *History of the Mexican War*. Edited by Mary Rachel Wilcox. Washington, D.C.: The Church News Publishing Company, 1892.

Williams, William Appleman. *From Colony to Empire: Essays in the History of American Foreign Relations*. New York: John Wiley & Sons, Inc., 1937.

Winders, Bruce. *Mr. Polk's Army: The American Military Experience in the Mexican War*. College Station: Texas A&M University Press, 1997.

INDEX

Hobsbawm, Eric, 97
Huasteca, 37-38, 88, 92, 94, 109
Huejutla de Reyes, 43, 94
Hughes, George Wurtz, 63
Hughes, John, 22
Humboldt, Alexander von, 4
Humphrey, Santiago, 35, 98
Illinois volunteer regiment, 26
Irrizarri, Juan Manuel, 71
Iturbide, Saba, 37
Jalisco, state of, 18, 37-39, 70
Jarauta, Celedonio de, 37, 39, 69, 87, 148
Jehlen, Myra, 151
Jimenez, José Maria, 37
Jomini, Antoine Henri, 21-22
Juárez, Benito, 115, 149
Kearney, Philip, 47
Kenly, John Reese, 58
Keough, David, viii
Kerr, Omi, ix
Kirkham, Ralph W., 145
La Paz, 65
Ladd, Horatio O., 146
Lally, Folliot T., 43, 94-96
Lander, Ernest McPherson, 146
Lane, Joseph, 62, 65, 118
Las Animas, xvi
Las Vigas, xvi
Lee, Robert E., 99
Levy, Sara, ix
light corps, attacks on convoys 41-45, 114-118; attacks on other forces 45-49; formation of 35-40
limpieza de sangre, 3
Llorente, Anastasio, 38, 93
López de Santa Anna, Antonio, as general 17, 30, 55, 73-74; as president 13, 70, 87, 89
Mansfield, Edward D., 123, 145
Marcy, William Learned, 42, 69
Marroqui, Joaquin, 38
Martin, James Kirby, vii

Mata, José María, 43
Matamoros, Felix, 38
Matamoros, state of Tamaulipas, 23, 27, 67
Mazipil, 100
McAfee, Ward, 148
McDougall, Walter A., 151
McIntosh, James S., 42
Meade, George Gordon, 26
Mejares, Antonio, 65
Mendez, Elutherio, 38
Metlatonoc, 49
Mexico City, battle for, 59-60
México, state of, xv, 13, 18-19, 23, 37, 39, 78, 88, 110
Meyer, Brantz, 145
Michoacán, state of, 12, 18-19, 38-39, 49-51, 72, 149
Miles, Dixon H., 64
Miñón, José Vicente, 16, 102
Moderados, 10, 75
Moinafuentes, Juan Maria, 38
Molino del Rey, 54
Montano, Manuel, 38, 87
Montano, Miguel, 50
Monterosa, Doroteo, 54
Monterrey, 16-19, 23, 65, 93, 98-99, 106
Mora, José María Luis, 7, 12
Morelos, state of, xv, 38
Musick, Michael, viii
Nasadro, José Ignacio, 38
National Bridge (Puente Nacional), 42-44, 61
Nebel, Carlos, 113
Nuevo León, state of, xvi, 19, 23, 31, 37, 39, 54, 66, 106, 109, 114-115
Nunez, Gabriel, 38
Oaxaca, state of, 12, 18, 39-40
Obregon, Pablo, 38
O'Brien, Thomas F., vii
Ocampo, Melchor, 149
Olanez, Miguel Hernandez, 38
Ometepec, state of Oaxaca, 50